THE JOB OF THE CEO

Waldemar Schmidt

Editora Val de Mar

THE JOB OF THE CEO

A Lifelong Career Guide for Future, Present and Retiring CEOs

© 2020 Waldemar Schmidt & Editora Val de Mar

Book design: The Author & Marianne Gulstad, Publizon
Printed by CreateSpace, An Amazon.com Company

2nd edition July 2020
ISBN 978-29700884-6-2

Published by Editora Val de Mar
www.editoravaldemar.com
CEO@editoravaldemar.com

TABLE OF CONTENTS

I DEDICATE
THE JOB OF THE CEO
TO
FUTURE, PRESENT AND RETIRING CEOs
OF ALL GENDERS,
AGES, NATIONALITIES AND CULTURES
IN COMPANIES
OF ALL SIZES AND
ALL KINDS OF OWNERSHIP

AND

TO ANYONE INTERESTED IN
LEADERSHIP AND MANAGEMENT

PREFACE

This is the second edition of THE JOB OF THE CEO. I continue to listen and learn. Also to my readers, wherefore I have addressed their feed-back. The biggest change is that I have made it much clearer that the book is a lifelong career guide for future, present and retiring CEOs. I have also made an effort to make my many lessons learnt clearer.

50 years in CEO and chairman roles with expensive failures and rewarding successes have taught me many valuable leadership lessons. I have gathered the essence of these lessons in THE JOB OF THE CEO with the ambition that I can inspire others to find their own ways to a long and successful CEO career.

The flow in THE JOB OF THE CEO is organized in chronological order:

- Understanding THE JOB OF THE CEO
- Determining whether THE JOB OF THE CEO is right for you
- Career planning
- Getting onto the CEO career ladder and staying there
- Retiring from your last CEO job to pursue a post-CEO career

Each chapter is a stand-alone chapter, which means that there deliberately are many overlaps in the book.

How you read the book will depend on where you are in your career. Here is our guidance as to which chapters you should focus on before you read the entire book:

- Future CEOs: 1—13 and 22—24
- Present CEOs: 10—14, 17—18 and 22—24
- Retiring CEOs: 15—16, 19—21 and 24

The book is NOT for skimming and speed-reading. Read slowly, reflect, be inspired and make notes that are relevant to your career. Keep the hard copy by your side at all times and the Kindle version on the go.

You will notice that I never apply 'MBH—Management By Hope' as a management style. But I will make an exception: It is my sincere **hope** that THE JOB OF THE CEO will put you in the right 'mood', *inspire* you and *guide* you to find your own way to a long and successful CEO career.

Waldemar Schmidt

The below career chart is designed to help you navigate successfully through your entire career. My career path is included for your guidance:

THE CEO CAREER PATH CHART: WALDEMAR SCHMIDT

FUTURE CEOs	PRESENT CEOs	RETIRING CEOs
AGE: 25–29	AGE: 29–60	AGE: 60–80+
WORKING HOURS/YEAR: 3,000	WORKING HOURS/YEAR: 3,000	WORKING HOURS/YEAR: 2,000 → 1,500 → 0
YEARS IN JOBS:	YEARS IN JOBS:	YEARS IN JOBS:
KNOW YOUR CUSTOMERS: ☐ Sales ☐ Marketing ☐ Customer service	CEO JOBS: ☑ S – Small ☑ M – Medium	SECOND CAREER: ☑ Chairman role ☑ Board member ☑ Other roles
KNOW YOUR PRODUCTS: ☑ Operations ☑ Manufacturing ☑ Supply chain ☐ Technology	☑ L – Large ☑ XL – Extra large ☐ XXL – Forbes Global 2000 company	THIRD CAREER: ☑ Board roles ☑ Investor ☑ Mentor ☑ Speaker & writer ☑ Pro-bono roles
KNOW YOUR NUMBERS: ☐ Accounting ☐ Business control ☐ Management consultancy (Strategy and operations) ☑ Junior management positions	AN UNEXPECTED EVENT MAKES YOU: ☐ CEO – because you were there as CFO, COO or board member	RETIREMENT: ☑ Pro-bono roles ☑ Investor ☑ Mentor ☐ Other: ☐ No more business roles

CHAPTER 1

THE JOB OF THE CEO

INTRODUCTION

"THE JOB OF THE CEO is a wonderful job,
if you master it.
But if you do not,
it is all but wonderful"

If you dream of becoming a CEO, you must understand THE JOB OF THE CEO and what CEOs do. And you must find out whether THE JOB OF THE CEO is right for you.

The purpose of this chapter is to give you our practical insights into THE JOB OF THE CEO and to inspire you to become a great leader. Being a great leader is the platform you need to become a successful CEO over a long period. We will give you our best advise, but we will remind you that there is no simple formula to becoming a successful CEO.

When we talk about CEOs and THE JOB OF THE CEO we do not only talk about CEOs of large global groups. We talk about anyone with a CEO job. There are hundreds of thousands of exiting CEO jobs out there, ranging from the CEO of your own one-person company to being the CEO of a large global group as we show in the next chart:

SIZE	DESCRIPTION
S	CEO of your own one-person company CEO of a small local company Country CEO of small operation
M	Country CEO of mid-sized operation CEO of a small group Regional CEO of small group
L	Country CEO of large operation Divisional CEO of large operation CEO of a mid-sized group
XL	Country CEO of large operation Divisional CEO of large operation CEO of a mid-sized group
XXL	Forbes Global 2000 company

2020 © Waldemar Schmidt

WHAT CEOs DO

It is very often said that the purpose of business is to make money and to create sustainable wealth for shareholders. However, we hold the view that successful CEOs do not only manage their companies by the principles of shareholder value; they take a much more holistic approach to their job by applying a stakeholder approach. The rationale for this is that you cannot create value for your shareholders in the long run, if you do not at the same time treat your entire stakeholders (customers, employees, suppliers, the environment and broader society) well.

Put simply, CEOs have three key tasks: #1) Set the direction, i.e. develop strategies with their teams; #2) Identify, recruit, develop and retain talented people; and #3) Execute strategies with their teams.

WHAT CEOs do is universal and does not depend on culture. HOW they do it may depend on the local culture and other circumstances. The appraisal of a CEO's performance should be based on performance and on the management style with which they perform.

CEO TASK #1 IS SETTING THE DIRECTION: Great leaders have the ability to create a shared vision about what kind of company they want to create together with their teams. Great leaders make sure that the vision of the company becomes deeply rooted in the organization, kept 'fresh' and dynamic. They are also very good at identifying the values upon which the company should be built and developed. With a shared vision as the guiding star and with sound and well understood values in place, they take the initiative to develop an exciting long-term strategy through a top-down/bottom-up team planning process in which they play the role of leader and coach. The key to a successful strategy is to involve as many people as possible in the planning process. Our learnings about how you should see strategy is illustrated in the chart, The CEOs Strategy Planning Concept.

Group CEOs are very much in charge of strategy development and they work closely with their boards and their direct reports in a dynamic team planning process. The direct reports, including regional CEOs and other senior executives, also work with their teams to contribute to strategy development. This concept continues all the way down the hierarchy (top/down) and then up (bottom/up). Many CEOs like to be supported by an internal strategy team and at occasions by strategy consultants. That is fine as long as they remain in charge and let the advisors advise.

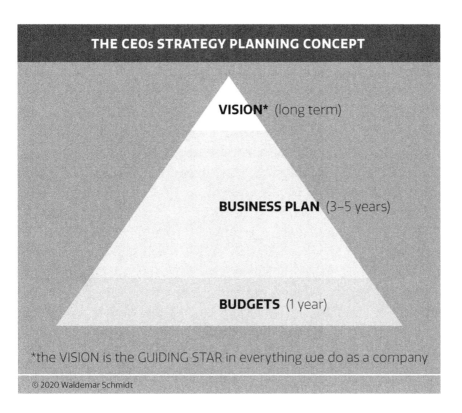

THE CEOs STRATEGY PLANNING CONCEPT

VISION* (long term)

BUSINESS PLAN (3–5 years)

BUDGETS (1 year)

*the VISION is the GUIDING STAR in everything we do as a company

© 2020 Waldemar Schmidt

Research shows that only 20% of companies stick to their strategy over long periods, and that 80% have changed their strategy in the last 12 months. This is not because the strategies constantly have to be changed due to disruptive events. It is mostly because their strategies were never deeply rooted in the organization.

If the CEO keeps coming up with new strategies all the time, the organization will discover and therefore just carry on as they have always done. Research also shows that the average lifetime of CEOs is three to five years. The combination of ever changing strategies and CEOs can only lead to poor performance.

Successful CEOs do not change their strategies all the time, and they stay in their jobs for lengthy periods. Successful CEOs understand that strategies must be clear, meaningful to and deeply rooted in the organization. In companies where the strategy is clear, meaningful and deeply rooted in the organization, the strategy will not come and go with the CEO. Successful CEOs make sure that they keep their strategy 'fresh' at all times, watch out for disruptive competition and if appropriate develop new disruptive strategies.

Great leaders have a strategic instinct and an ability to drive and inspire the organization whilst driving the strategy process with their teams. They are inspiring story tellers with a natural ability to communicate their vision and strategy to employees and all other important stakeholders, including investors. Great leaders give their people a sense of purpose, i.e. why their job and contribution, is important for the success of the business.

Developing a great strategy is more art than science. It is not an analytical exercise. You can often choose between two or more equally great strategies. The one that you decide to go for, with good judgement, will be the best and the one that you should execute relentlessly with your organization.

Formulating strategy is an absolute key task of CEOs.

CEO TASK #2 IS TO ASSEMBLE GREAT TEAMS: Great leaders understand that:

1. It takes great teams with talented people to run a business successfully
2. Diverse teams in terms of gender, nationality, culture, age, competencies, etc. perform better than teams that are not diverse

3. Diverse teams are fun to work with
4. It is often smart to recruit people that are smarter than themselves
5. It is essential to hire people with skills that are complementary to their own skills
6. They should not recruit clones of themselves

Great leaders organize their companies in a way that offers many jobs with a high degree of freedom, transparency and responsibility. This is the best way to discover and develop talent and to enhance performance.

Identifying, recruiting, developing and retaining great potential and mature leaders is probably the most difficult of the three CEO tasks. You can make all sorts of tests and get it wrong. You can interview alone or by committee and get it wrong. You can get it wrong by solely relying on your own judgement. If you do not ask tough questions when checking references, you can get it wrong. If you recruit candidates with the same characteristics and skills as yourself, you also go astray. Even using top search firms it is no guarantee of 100% hit rate. Recruitment of people with proven record of achievements in challenging jobs is what you must be looking for. In addition you must obtain certainty that they have a positive leadership style.

CEO TASK #3 IS EXECUTION: Great leaders instil a performance culture that encourages everybody to deliver based on a shared vision with clear objectives and strategies, and they act as playing coaches, helping the team with execution. Relentless execution of the agreed strategy is therefore another key CEO function. The distinction between a great leader and a not-so-great leader is often found in his or her ability to execute the strategy with the right kind of management style.

CEO TIME MANAGEMENT

How do successful CEOs spend their time and what do they actually do? There is no simple answer to this question. There is a huge difference between the ways in which a CEO of a small business spends his or her time, and how a CEO of a large publicly listed global group spends his or her time. Nevertheless, any CEO spends his or her time on the following:

- Show leadership 24/7 with focus on the three CEO tasks: strategy, people management and execution
- Away from the office 2—3 days a week learning, coaching and motivating people to execute the strategy and deliver results
- Hold regular meetings with the board and the team leaving space in the diary to be available for unplanned events
- Stay in close touch with all important stakeholders
- Spend one week each year attending seminars that provide inspiration, education and personal development

In summary, successful CEOs develop great strategies and stick to them for long periods, assemble great teams and execute almost to perfection. And remember CEOs are not only judged on their results. They are also judged on *how* they achieve their results.

DANGERS TO BE AWARE OF

With THE JOB OF THE CEO comes permanent attention and scrutiny. Among the things that you need to be aware of are:

1. People watch you 24/7. Everybody around you look for leadership, guidance, recognition, etc.
2. All stakeholders (including the media) put you under the microscope. Everybody has an opinion about you
3. Your colleagues and staff will change their behaviour towards you and make things look rosier than they perhaps are. They want to please you and make you look good even in situations where you do not deserve it
4. When you travel to visit subsidiaries you will probably only be shown the best and may therefore lose sight of what's really going on in your organization
5. You will be invited to all sorts of events. You should not get carried away and become a 'Celebrity CEO'. Be very selective as to external activities
6. Some sections of the media, politicians, NGOs and the general public often see CEOs as cynical and greedy 'fat cats' who are only driven by their own egos and who cynically operate under the guise of shareholder value. Unfortunately, this viewpoint is sometimes correct. You must avoid this
7. Be aware of rivalry and politics in your organization and deal with it when discovered
8. The CEO graveyard is littered with ex-CEOs who have gone from great leaders to 'Celebrity CEOs' and then the most reviled CEOs. The reason for this is often that arrogance and greed gradually creep in and turn successful CEOs into Celebrity CEOs who believe that normal rules no longer apply to them
9. Getting the job of the CEO is hard. Keeping the job of the CEO is even harder. Retiring from the job of the CEO is probably the hardest of all
10. Remain the person you were. But keep on learning and applying the lessons that you learn

CHAPTER 2

LEADERSHIP STYLES

It is our view that CEOs should not only be evaluated on their results. They must also be evaluated on their leadership style. It is clearly our experience that CEOs who are successful over a long period have a "positive" leadership style. There many terms that are used to describe leadership styles. We show some of them and the impact that they have on long-term results:

LEADERSHIP STYLES		
NEGATIVE	**NEUTRAL**	**POSITIVE**
Autocratic	Abdication	Coaching
Bureaucratic	Charismatic	Democratic
Command & Control	Hands-off	Empowerment
Control freak	Laissez-faire	Focused
Dictatorial	Management by hope	Marathon Runner
Machiavelli		MBO-Management by objectives
Micro management		Strategic
Sprinter		Team-oriented
Unfocussed		Visionary

2020 © Waldemar Schmidt

There is one situation where the "positive" leader will have to apply an autocratic leadership style. That is when the company faces a major crisis. In such situations speed and very strong leadership is essential. There is no time for off-site team sessions. The CEO must change his or her leadership style to autocratic until the crisis is over.

CHAPTER 3

WHAT MAKES A GREAT LEADER

I have through observations, expensive failures and rewarding successes learnt a great deal about leadership, leaders and what you must look for when you recruit, develop and retain leaders. My experiences are practical, non-analytical and non-academic.

The objective of this chapter is to:

1. Make future CEOs understand what it takes for them to become great leaders and become successful CEOs
2. Help senior executives what to focus on when recruiting and promoting CEOs to work for them

Identifying leaders and potential leaders, developing and retaining them is a crucial and very difficult CEO task. You can make all sorts of tests and get it wrong. You can interview alone or by committee and get it wrong. You can get it wrong by solely relying on your judgement. If you do not ask tough questions when checking references on new people, you can get it wrong. If you recruit candidates with the same characteristics and skills as yourself, you also go astray. Even using top search firms is no guarantee of 100%-hit rates. Recruitment of people with a proven record of accomplishments (results and positive management style) in challenging jobs is what you must be looking for. What is more, they have what we would sum-up as 'the right attitude'. Our experience clearly shows that micromanagers and control freaks do not have the right attitude and rarely produce great results over long periods.

In the following, we will discuss some of the key qualities of great leaders.

1—GREAT LEADERS ARE BORN AND MADE

I have during my long business life learnt that we all are BORN with a certain amount of Leadership DNA. In any group of people, young or old anywhere in the world one will emerge as a leader; i.e. is MADE a leader when the group faces a challenge. The leader that emerges will typically: 1) Take the initiative to find a solution, 2) Make the group work as a team and 3) Solve the problem with the team. This is exactly what leadership is about.

It is my experience that nobody is BORN with 0 Leadership DNA points. Is it also my experience that nobody is BORN with 100 Leadership points. But I do believe that great leaders have an upper quartile amount of raw leadership DNA, which has been identified and developed over time through early and demanding jobs with responsibility for people, customers, and profit and loss ideally in different cultures and in different business cycles. It is about getting roles that stretch you as a person as much as possible in the earliest stages of your career. Learning and applying your lessons will gradually push you Leadership DNA to its limit.

My lessons learnt about whether leaders are born or made is illustrated in te below figure:

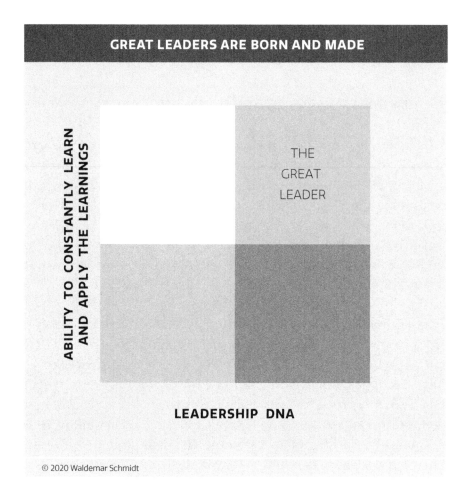

2 – GREAT LEADERS HAVE HIGH IQ AND EQ

I have worked with executives with very different levels of EQ and IQ. My experience is that great leaders have upper quartile EQ and IQ. But very importantly that EQ is higher than IQ.

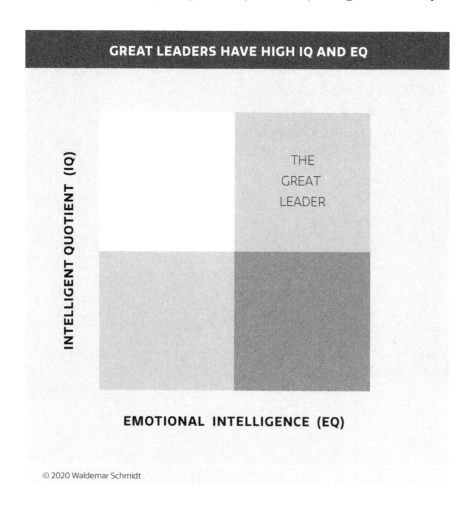

© 2020 Waldemar Schmidt

3 – CHARACTERISICS OF GREAT LEADERS

My experience with successes and failures has taught me that great leaders who become successful CEOs also have very specific characteristics including:

KEY CHARACTERISTICS OF GREAT LEADERS

1. Passion for people
2. Strong team player
3. Very high level of emotional intelligence (EQ > IQ)
4. Very high level of energy
5. Balanced personality
6. Sound judgement
7. Curious and eager to learn
8. Integrity and ethical standards
9. Great listeners
10. Seems lucky

© 2016 Waldemar Schmidt

4 — SKILLS OF GREAT LEADERS

My experience with successes and failures has taught me that great leaders who become successful CEOs have developed very specific skills. We have developed the below list with 10 skills that in our opinion typify great leaders:

KEY SKILLS OF GREAT LEADERS

1. Takes initiative and shoulders responsibility
2. Strategic thinker
3. Excellent communicator with people at all levels
4. Reliable: produces results and makes money
5. Interested in all business functions
6. Has intimate knowledge of the business and understands what drives it
7. Understands the big picture and the detail equally well
8. Does not complicate matters — keeps them simple
9. Removes roadblocks
10. Makes sound decisions

© 2016 Waldemar Schmidt

5 – GREAT LEADERS WORK HARD AND SMART

THE JOB OF THE CEO is not for lazy people. It is hard word. Based on my personal experience and observations of others I have learnt many lessons about great leaders' workloads:

PEOPLE WHO BECOME GREAT GLOBAL LEADERS HAVE BEEN WILLING ENROUTE TO PUT UP WITH AND ENJOY:

1. Working 60 – 70 hours a week
2. Often prioritising work over family life
3. Living abroad for several years (with their families), learning new languages and developing knowledge of new cultures
4. Taking responsibility and working under high levels of stress
5. Handling very difficult personnel issues
6. Trusting people
7. Sacrificing pay in their early career if necessary
8. Taking on very different positions to learn all aspects of business
9. Making decisions that are respected, but not popular with their colleagues
10. Not always getting the promotion, pay and titles they had hoped for

© 2016 Waldemar Schmidt

SUMMARY

If you dream of becoming a CEO, we recommend that carry out our self-assessment test in Chapter 5 or on our website www.editoravaldemar.com to evaluate the results and to determine whether the job of the CEO is right for you.

CHAPTER 4

EXAMPLES OF SUCCESSFUL CEOs' EDUCATION, NATIONALITY AND CAREER PATHS

EDUCATION

Many kinds of education can lead to THE JOB OF THE CEO.

THE JOB OF THE CEO is not an academic job. But you must have an above-average level of intelligence and a decent education. Your IQ does not need to meet the requirements of the MENSA society (the top 2%. Your EQ (emotional intelligence) must be in the upper quartile.

Typically, you will have 12—13 years of regular school ending with an A-level, Baccalaureate, IB—International Baccalaureate or similar followed by 3—5 years at university, graduating with a bachelor's or master's degree. Some top up their education with an MBA degree.

If you want to pursue a career in business, you often have had extensive relevant work experiences whilst at college.

A top degree from an Ivy League university will almost certainly secure a promising career in academia, the public sector, consulting, investment banking etc. However, it will not necessarily lead to a successful CEO career.

When we look at the educational background of CEOs in large global firms, we have noted some geographical patterns. In the UK, many CEOs have a degree in accounting and have been CFOs before they become CEOs. In Sweden and Germany, many CEOs are engineers. In France, CEOs have often have studied political science at the École des Hautes Études Commerciales in Paris and spent their early career in the public sector. In the US, many CEOs have degrees in business and marketing. Such examples illustrate that there is no standard education for CEOs and that the pattern in the countries mentioned is related to the business structure in those countries. Sweden and Germany have large engineering companies. The UK is the financial centre of Europe. In France there are many state-owned or state-controlled companies. The USA is home to the world's largest global FMCG — Fast Moving Consumer Goods companies.

Education and learning at school and university is not the end of your acquisition of knowledge if you want to pursue your career dreams of becoming a global CEO. Learning takes on a whole new dimension once you start working. Learning is a life-long occupation; you will never become too old or too wise to learn. You will learn by working with smart and competent bosses and colleagues, by attending relevant courses, by reading, by being curious, by asking questions and by trial and error during work.

NATIONALITY: When global companies from the old world used to be called international companies and subsequently multinational companies, many of them employed their own nationals as expatriates in most key positions in every foreign country. The reason for this must have had to do with issues such as control, trust, values, transfer of business knowhow, and often a lack of local talent. Many large multinationals had hundreds of expatriates of their own nationality posted around the world. This concept has changed and is continuing to change because of on-going globalization. Global companies have discovered that diversity works very well, and that local talent is available. There is also a cost issue. Posting an expatriate with family to a foreign country is very expensive compared with employing a local person. Furthermore, having expensive expatriates working side-by-side with locals in similar jobs is not positive for the working climate. Disparities in pay and conditions can breed resentment.

When considering the way in which global companies from the new world go about their global expansion, it appears that they often post managers from their home country in key positions around the world, including countries in the old world, where talent is available.

Nonetheless, the trend is clear. In the future, what counts is talent and not nationality. When looking at the nationalities of CEOs in an increasing number of large global companies around the world, we see a trend where more and more CEOs are foreign nationals. The future CEOs and management teams of successful global companies will be true 'Citizens of the World'!

CAREER PATHS: There is not just one avenue that will lead you to the job of the CEO. Our experience has shown that your career path is a result of a number of interlinked factors, including the opportunities you identified or you have been given, your achievements and the choices that you make and unexpected opportunities that suddenly appear.

We have identified that there are certain pre-CEO jobs that you should have to facilitate your path to a CEO job:

We have often seen that people, who have had impressive leadership careers, were catapulted into leadership positions early on by someone who believed in them. However, there are still some tried and tested career pathways that can enhance your chances of a CEO job as opposed to merely relying on circumstances.

CAREER WITH A GLOBAL BLUE-CHIP COMPANY: Join 'the right company' directly after graduation or well before the age of 35 years. Your first job will typically be in finance, sales/marketing, supply chain or operations. In a graduate programme, you typically start with one or two different specialist jobs at HQ over a 3—5 year period. After the specialist jobs, you will probably be offered a junior management position abroad and then if you deserve it your first small CEO job. After your first small CEO job and a bigger/big CEO job abroad, you should be ready for a senior POSITION at HQ. Level-2 or 3. Take your time to consider your options. Waiting for the top CEO job in the group to become available is a very risky proposition. You therefore have two options: continue as one of the number two or three men or women in your group or try to become CEO of a smaller group in an industry similar to yours. If you are prepared to take on a higher risk, you can try a 'double switch', i.e. change of industry and move up the ladder to become CEO in a different industry.

THE CFO TRACK: Typically starts with a degree in accountancy working for one of the global accounting firms after which you join a client firm (or another firm) where you have one or two financial specialist jobs until you are about 35. At that age you should be with 'the right company' to advance through roles such as treasurer, internal auditor, business controller, CFO of small operation, CFO of medium and larger operations in different countries. When you are about 45—50, you may then move to the CFO position at group level, or if you are in the UK you may be ready for a CEO job. CFOs sometimes become CEOs as a default solution, if something unforeseen happens with the sitting CEO and the board needs a quick solution. An alternative to becoming group CFO could maybe be to become CEO of a large country within your group, which will help position you as a credible candidate for the group CEO position if or when it becomes available. In case you see no prospects of your dream job becoming a realistic option for you, you may prefer to leave your company and become CFO of a larger company in your industry or in another industry. CFO positions are not as tied to one particular industry, as are CEO jobs. You may therefore decide to go for the more risky alternatives, such as a CEO job of a smaller company in your industry, or to make a double switch and become CEO in a smaller company in a new industry.

MULTI-COMPANY CAREER: There are CEOs who after their pre-CEO jobs for a variety of reasons, end up having many short lived CEO jobs in many companies in many different industries. The probability for such people to end their careers as long-term successful CEOs is not very high. Some do, however succeed as serial turn-around CEOs, interim CEOs or CEOs of private equity portfolio companies. Multi-company CEO careers are normally not the results of careful career planning.

ENTREPRENEURS: People mostly become entrepreneurs because they have great ideas and want the freedom of being their own masters and not having bosses. We distinguish between two kinds of entrepreneurs. The classic entrepreneur is the 'built to last' entrepreneur. Sometimes he or she goes through two or three ideas before finding the right project. Then there is the 'built to exit' entrepreneur of which there are many in the IT and internet industry. The motives of the two types of entrepreneurs seem to be quite different. The serial entrepreneur seems to be more motivated by money than the classic entrepreneur is. They typically talk a lot about 'exit' all the time. If you have the urge to become an entrepreneur, try it out as early as you can and decide what kind of entrepreneur you want to be. Make a business plan to guide your company and your career and to raise the funds that you need. If you are successful with the execution of your project, fine; if not, make a new career plan and embark on a career as a corporate worker and try to be in your industry of choice when you are about 35 years old. The experience as an entrepreneur can be a very valuable asset on your CV, if you have learnt something important. There are people who become entrepreneurs by accident, which typically happens if they get involved in an MBO (Management Buy Out) opportunity. To make a judgement about joining an MBO is not only about the fascination of developing a business: you and your family must also make very important decisions about your private finances because you will need to invest. Are you and your partner willing to take a bank loan with collateral in your home? The step from corporate worker is risky but can be very rewarding depending on the 'exit', i.e. the sale of your company. If it goes really well for you, you may have made enough money to become a business angel or an entrepreneur. If the exit is not successful, you may have two problems: a financial problem and a career problem, i.e. who will employ you after a failed or an unsuccessful MBO? Planning a career as a CEO entrepreneur is complex.

FAMILY BUSINESS: We will discuss three different situations here. The first situation is where owners want a family member to be the CEO generation after generation. We have observed that it is unlikely that the founder's family forever can produce successful CEOs. If your family expects you to become the next CEO after your father or your uncle, we recommend that you as a minimum do two things. Firstly, perform our self-assessment tests and talk with experts about your suitability for a CEO job. Secondly, if you are deemed suitable you should work in a couple of relevant pre-CEO jobs outside your family business to acquire the competencies that are needed for its future success.

The second situation is for people who consider working for family-owned or family-controlled businesses. Many family companies are extremely well run, have strong values and therefore want family members to hold the key jobs in their firms. This means that you will have to decide whether you want to join a company where it is highly unlikely that you will have a chance to become its CEO.

The third situation is where the owners of family business decide to recruit an external CEO. They are sometimes tempted to recruit a top executive from one of their global competitor. This commonly poses a very serious problem. The top executive from the large global firm is a 'corporate worker', who has advanced through the ranks in a business environment where the company was run as a matrix organization and multiple support functions were the norm. The transition to a family-owned company with hands-on management is often unsuccessful for both parties.

THE CONSULTING TRACK: This path to a CEO job is typically one where you join a global strategy consulting firm after university or after your MBA degree and stay there for 3—5 years. Having worked with and advised CEOs in client firms, you may start thinking about a career move from advising to executing. Your experience from a highly demanding and professional environment gives you a unique perspective of business and usually a very valuable insight into one or two particular industries and a valuable toolbox. You also develop a network with colleagues and clients that can serve you very well throughout your business career. You go through our self-assessment tests and draft a career plan for the path to your dream job. You get yourself a job where your skills can be deployed and tell your new employer what your dream job is. If at all possible, you become part of its fast track programme and become one of their 'high potentials'. The most obvious first role is in the strategy function or in the M&A department. If you show sufficient interest, the right people skills, etc., it is likely that your next job in the company will be one where you get P&L and people responsibility. Your new job could also be one where you have been part of the team that worked on a business strategy project for the client—which you will be asked to execute. You have now had your pre-CEO career. You have stepped onto the pre-CEO career ladder and may benefit from our career advise below. There are also many examples where senior partners from consulting firms with high level of EQ become successful CEOs.

FROM MAIL ROOM TO BOARD ROOM: One and more generation ago, it was not unusual that you could join a firm as an apprentice or trainee right out of school and move all the way up to the CEO—and even to the chairman position. There are still some companies, such as banks and shipping companies, that follow this path, and which typically provide on-going and adequate management training relevant to their industry. Some even sponsor high potentials for their MBA degree. However, even with such well-established programs in place, these companies often feel that they need to complement their home-grown talent for the very top jobs. Accordingly, this track is no longer a safe track for people who dream of a top CEO job.

MBAs: An MBA degree has the potential to accelerate your career towards a CEO job. As an MBA graduate, you may start with a large consulting firm where you end up being offered a job with a client company, or you may join a large global company in strategy/business development, after which you gradually move up the ladder until you may be ready for a CEO job. Some MBAs become entrepreneurs and therefore CEOs of their own companies.

ENGINEERS: You typically start your career in a specialist function such as operations or supply chain and gradually rise to a junior management position with responsibility for people and budgets if you demonstrate initiative and leadership talent. You may then move to a customer facing function, which will add to the skills that you need, if you want to become a CEO. If you do well during your pre-CEO career, your chances of getting on the CEO track have improved immensely.

ACCOUNTANTS: After a shorter or longer period with the audit-firm that you have trained with, an opportunity to be employed by a client may arise. Probably in a finance function to begin with. If you dream of becoming a CEO there may be two ways to go about this. You can grow into the CFO job and be ready to move into the CEO job, if it becomes available. Or you can try to follow our pre-CEO job advise with your new employer and then get your first CEO there.

SUMMARY: Common for people who have risen to a CEO job is that they have shown initiative, results and leadership talent with the right attitude and management style, after which they have been given increasingly bigger opportunities to show what they are capable of. Employers will generally spot a talented person and give him or her a chance to show his or her leadership potential.

CHAPTER 5

HOW TO ASSESS WHETHER THE JOB OF THE CEO IS RIGHT FOR YOU

If you have read and understood Chapters 1, 2 and 3 you should now have a good understanding of the CEO job, the characteristics, skills and career paths of people who become successful CEOs. You have learnt which opportunities and challenges you will face on your way to your dream job.

Whether your dream is to become a CEO or whether you are not certain, if a CEO career is right for you, it is now time to get an understanding of your potential to become a great leader. You should therefore carry out our self-assessment tests, reflect on the results and make a decision about your career. Whatever decision you make, it will have a major impact on the rest of your professional as well as your private life.

The self-assessment tests are entirely empirical. They are developed by the author based on his long career as a global businessman with extensive CEO and chairman experience. The tests are meant to give you guidance. They will not give you black and white answers.

The tests are designed for potential global CEOs. However, as we live in a global world, even a local company will have "foreign" customers, suppliers, staff, shareholders. If you are determined to stay local, the career tests are still relevant. You may accordingly be a little soft, when you evaluate the results of some of your tests.

Whatever your dreams are, we suggest that you sit down with a person, who knows you really well, and work through the five tests. This person should be a mentor, a senior colleague or a search consultant with whom you already have established a relationship. Your partner should also have a say. The people who help you with this assessment must be brutally honest, frank and objective—and you must be honest with yourself. If you cheat you only cheat yourself and this is not good for your career and for your family life. Embarking on a CEO career without having what it takes, without support of your partner and without being willing to do what it takes, can only lead to frustration.

We suggest that you visit our website and print this chapter www.editoravaldemar.com and that you use the printed tests rather than the tests of the book. As already mentioned, the tests are not analytical. They are *empirical judgement tests.*

The combined result of all your assessment tests will probably fall into three categories:

PASSED—Every indication is that you **do** have what it takes to become a CEO

MAYBE—The result is not clear

FAILED—It is very clear that you **do not** have what it takes to become a CEO

Even if you 'fail' in one or more of the self-assessment tests, we recommend that you complete all of them. Completing all tests and evaluating the results together with your mentor will be valuable for your future career, even if you decide not to pursue a CEO path. Reflecting over the results you may well be able to improve on some of your weak spots once you become aware of them.

THE SELF–ASSESSMENT TESTS

SELF–ASSESSMENT TEST **NO.1**

WHY DO YOU WANT TO BECOME A CEO?

This test is not for you if you are certain that a CEO job is not what you want. However, it is good for you to know about this test when you start your business career.

TEST 1	MY MOTIVE TO BECOME A CEO IS:	
TYPE A:	I am primarily driven by the urge to prove my abilities and to work in a team	☐
TYPE B:	I am primarily driven by money and power	☐
Result:	PASSED ☐ FAILED ☐	

Comments from my mentor, my partner and myself:

If you honestly feel that you are a Type A person, you have passed test 1 and should go to the next tests.

If you are a Type B person, we suggest that you also complete all remaining tests and at the end seriously consider your options. If your prime motive really is money, power and recognition you should revisit the options we mention under MULTI COMPANY CAREER.

SELF–ASSESSMENT TEST **NO.2**
ARE YOU WILLING TO DO WHAT IT TAKES TO BECOME A GLOBAL CEO?

The second test is about 'sacrifices' that you must be willing to make. Ideally, you should not see them as sacrifices, because you love what you do and you learn so much. See test 2.

If you want to become a global CEO, you must ideally find all 10 items exciting and natural to deserve a YES. Just a few MAYBEs is a concern. If you have just one NO, you should carefully consider whether a career as a global CEO career is right for you and your partner.

If your ambition is to become a local CEO, you may have a NO on items 3 and 6.

TEST 2	AM I WILLING TO MAKE 'SACRIFICES' SUCH AS:	YES	NO	MAYBE	Comments:
1	Working 60–70 hours a week				
2	Often prioritising work over family life and hobbies				
3	Living abroad for several years (with your family), learning new languages and developing knowledge of new cultures				
4	Taking responsibility and work under high levels of stress				
5	Handling very difficult personnel issues				
6	Trusting people of different cultures				
7	Sacrificing pay in your early career if necessary				
8	Taking on very different positions to learn all aspects of business				
9	Making decisions that are not popular with people around you				
10	Not always getting the promotion, pay and titles as quickly as you had hoped for				
Result	How was your score?				

Result: PASSED ☐ FAILED ☐ MAYBE ☐

Comments from my mentor, my partner and myself:

DO YOU HAVE THE KEY CHARACTERISTICS
OF A GREAT LEADER?

The third test is about your characteristics and is a very deep and honest assessment of yourself on each of the 10 characteristics of a great leader:

TEST 3	DO I HAVE THE KEY CHARATERISTICS OF A GREAT LEADER?	POINTS 0-10	Comments:
1	Passion for people		
2	Strong team player		
3	Very high level of emotional intelligence (EQ > IQ)		
4	Very high level of energy		
5	Balanced personality		
6	Sound judgement		
7	Curious and eager to learn		
8	Integrity and high ethical standards		
9	Great listener		
10	Seems lucky		
Result: How was your score?		0–5: 6–7: 8–10:	PASSED ☐ FAILED ☐ MAYBE ☐

Comments from my mentor, my partner and myself:

Nobody is perfect, so we do not expect you to score 8', 9' or 10' on all. A few 6' or 7' are acceptable: But scores below 5' mean that the CEO job is not right for you.

DO YOU HAVE THE SKILLS OF A GREAT LEADER?

The fourth test is about your skills and is a very deep and honest assessment of yourself on each of the 10 characteristics of a great leader:

TEST 4	DO I HAVE THE KEY SKILLS OF A GREAT LEADER?	POINTS 0-10	Comments :
1	Takes initiative and shoulders responsibility		
2	Strategic thinker		
3	Excellent communicator with people at all levels		
4	Reliable: Produces results		
5	Interested in all business functions		
6	Has intimate knowlede of the business and understands what drives it		
7	Understands the big picture and the detail equally well		
8	Does not complicate matters – keeps them simple		
9	Removes road blocks		
10	Makes sound decisions		
Result: How was your score?		0–5: 6–7: 8–10:	PASSED ☐ FAILED ☐ MAYBE ☐

Comments from my mentor, my partner and myself:

Again, nobody is perfect, so we do not expect you to score 10x10. A few 6' or 7' are acceptable. Scores below 5' indicate that the CEO job is not right for you.

DO YOU HAVE RIGHT EQ/IQ BALANCE?

The fifth test is about the two dimensions of intelligence. Both IQ and EQ can be measured. However, for the purpose of this test we suggest that *sound judgement* is applied.

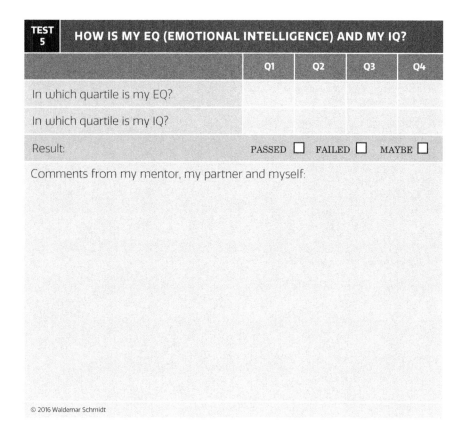

TEST 5	HOW IS MY EQ (EMOTIONAL INTELLIGENCE) AND MY IQ?			
	Q1	Q2	Q3	Q4
In which quartile is my EQ?				
In which quartile is my IQ?				
Result:	PASSED ☐ FAILED ☐ MAYBE ☐			
Comments from my mentor, my partner and myself:				

© 2016 Waldemar Schmidt

Our experience shows that great leaders typically have EQ and IQ in the 4th quartile. But EQ is higher than IQ.

SUMMARY OF YOUR SELF–ASSESSMENT TESTS:

Once you have completed and evaluated all 5 tests we suggest that you summarize the results to help you decide whether you have what it takes to be a great leader and to become a CEO with a long and successful career:

TEST NO.:	SELF-ASSESSMENT TEST REGARDING:	MY RESULTS:		
		PASSED	FAILED	MAYBE
1	My motive to become a CEO			
2	My willingness to make 'sacrifices'			
3	My leadership characteristics			
4	My leadership skills			
5	My EQ and IQ			
The overall result:				
Comments from my mentor, my partner and myself:				

If you are in the maybe area, we suggest that you consider planning a pre-CEO career to find out whether the CEO job could be right for you anyhow.

Whatever your results are, it is now time to reflect and *decide* if THE JOB OF THE CEO is right for you. Go to Chapter 6.

REFLECT, EVALUATE AND DECIDE WHETHER THE JOB OF THE CEO IS RIGHT FOR YOU

You are now at a crucial point in your career where your decision will have a very significant impact on your professional and private life. It is therefore very important that you make the right decision.

The self-assessment tests are empirical and not analytical nor academic. The tests are based on our many years of management experience. The tests give you an *indication* about whether the CEO job is right for you. Passing the test does however not guarantee that you will become a successful CEO over a very long period.

YOU HAVE PASSED THE TEST

You and your mentor have concluded that the results of the self-assessment tests indicate that you have what it takes and that you want to pursue a career that can lead to a CEO job. In addition, your partner supports the decision and you are both happy with the impact the decision will have on your work-life balance. The next steps will be that you start planning your career. We will discuss this in Chapters 8 — 12. When drawing up your career plan we suggest that you primarily focus on your pre-CEO career, how to get your first CEO job and on your dream CEO job. We suggest that you do aim too high. Aim at a S, M or L CEO job as your dream job. Do not aim at the top job in a Forbes 500 company.

YOU ARE IN THE AREA OF "MAYBE"?

If you are in doubt whether or not a CEO position is right for you, we recommend that you consider trying regardless. People with leadership potential typically learn and develop when given the opportunity to show their capabilities. You may have been too modest in your self-assessment. Give it a very serious attempt anyway. We recommend that you plan your pre-CEO career as if you were certain that the job of the CEO was right for you.

YOU HAVE CONCLUDED THAT THE CEO JOB IS NOT FOR YOU

If you have reached the conclusion that the CEO job is definitely not for you, we recommend that you start planning a career that is right for you.

Whatever the outcome of your self-assessment test, you should now move on to Chapters 7 — 12, which cover all key aspects of career planning. These chapters are tailored to people who want to pursue a CEO career; however, most of the advise should also inspire people who plan alternative careers.

Whatever you decide, it is very important that you find your own way to your dream job.

YOU ARE A FEMALE EXECUTIVE WITH AMBITIONS OF BECOMING A CEO AND RAISING A FAMILY

If you are a woman who has passed the test and you want to give priority to raising a family first, you should not despair. If you really want to become a CEO and raise a family, experience shows that the CFO path to the top can work very well. Consider developing a personal brand as a 'Commercial CFO with CEO potential.'

We have the following advise and comments about this situation:

1. Women are often also outstanding CFOs and move to CEO positions if the opportunity arises
2. A career break is not necessarily a big problem—even if your male colleagues race ahead of you
3. CFOs can change to another industry more easily than CEOs
4. Whilst raising a family, many employers will let you work from home on occasion and will understand that you are not ready for a transfer to a new country
5. Make an effort to work abroad very early on in your career
6. Female CFOs have higher chances of becoming CEOs than female HR, Legal and IT executives
7. Female CFOs are increasingly in demand as non-executive directors

YOU WANT TO BE AN ENTREPRENEUR AND CEO OF YOUR OWN BUSINESS

You want to be an entrepreneur driven by money, prestige and the business plan for the company that you want to create. The business plan should include all the key points that you most likely are familiar with. In addition and for your inspiration, we have drawn up a list of questions that we recommend you to carefully address:

1. Will you build a business to last or are you setting out to become a serial entrepreneur?
2. Ownership: Is it your intention to be the sole owner? Do you want to team up with a partner on 50/50 basis? Will you depend on external partners and if so what is the minimum stake that you want to own?
3. What will the impact be on the financial situation of you and your family?
4. What will the impact be on your work-life position?
5. How many years are you willing to spend until your business has proven its viability?
6. Will you be willing to step down from the CEO position if you get to a point where you are no longer the right person for the job?

Whatever you decide about your career, it is very important that you find your own path to your dream job as an entrepreneur.

START OF YOUR CAREER

WE suggest that you map out the path to your dream job, i.e. your pre-CEO jobs, the your first and second CEO jobs using the career chart:

THE CEO CAREER PATH CHART

FUTURE CEOs	PRESENT CEOs	RETIRING CEOs
AGE: 25–35/40	AGE: 35/40–60/65	AGE: 60/65–70/80
WORKING HOURS/YEAR: 3,000	WORKING HOURS/YEAR: 3,000	WORKING HOURS/YEAR: 2,000 ➜ 1,000 ➜ 0
YEARS IN JOBS: 10–15	YEARS IN JOBS: 20–30	YEARS IN JOBS: 10–20
KNOW YOUR CUSTOMERS: ☐ Sales ☐ Marketing ☐ Customer service	CEO JOBS: ☐ S – Small ☐ M – Medium	SECOND CAREER: ☐ Chairman role ☐ Board member ☐ Other roles
KNOW YOUR PRODUCTS: ☐ Operations ☐ Manufacturing ☐ Supply chain ☐ Technology	☐ L – Large ☐ XL – Extra large ☐ XXL – Forbes Global 2000 company	THIRD CAREER: ☐ Board roles ☐ Investor ☐ Mentor ☐ Speaker & writer ☐ Pro-bono roles
KNOW YOUR NUMBERS: ☐ Accounting ☐ Business control ☐ Management consultancy (Strategy and operations) ☐ Junior management positions	AN UNEXPECTED EVENT MAKES YOU: ☐ CEO 　– because you were there as CFO, COO or board member	RETIREMENT: ☐ Pro-bono roles ☐ Investor ☐ Mentor ☐ Other: ☐ No more business roles

CHAPTER 7

PLANNING ANOTHER CAREER IF THE JOB OF THE CEO IS NOT RIGHT FOR YOU

THE JOB OF THE CEO is primarily written for future, present, and retiring CEOs. Chapters 7 — 10 might also inspire other C-suite executives and non-CEOs.

The job of the CEO is not the only interesting job in the world. There are many other very interesting jobs that you can have. To be successful with your career it is important that you have a clear idea about your dream job and that you plan what you need to do to get it.

The decision that you are making about your career will have a major impact on the rest of your life including your work-life balance. We therefore strongly recommend that you involve your partner as well as a mentor in your career planning.

You may have decided that the CEO job is not for you even before you read THE JOB OF THE CEO. Or you may have made your decision after having performed the self-assessment tests. Whatever the reason, you will be well advised to prepare a career plan that can lead you to your dream job. Before you start planning your career, it may be helpful to analyse how you came to the conclusion that a CEO career is NOT right for you.

REASONS FOR YOUR DECISION NOT TO BECOME A CEO:

1. The job of the CEO is too demanding
2. The job of the CEO is too risky
3. I don't have the ambition and the confidence
4. I am not a people manager
5. The work-life balance is not worth it
6. Other reasons

© 2016 Waldemar Schmidt

Reflections over the above should help you decide which kind of job would be right for you.

To help you prepare your career plan we suggest that you carefully answer questions such as:

QUESTIONS ABOUT YOUR DREAM JOB:

1. What is my dream job?
2. Why is this job my dream job?
3. Where?
4. Which industry?
5. What kind of company: Large, small, local, global, new, old, family-owned, public etc.?
6. My work-life balance?
7. Other questions?
8. Which are the jobs I need to have to get my dream job?

© 2016 Waldemar Schmidt

Once you have addressed the reasons and questions in the above charts, you should write your career plan as a roadmap to your dream job.

We propose that you now go to Chapters 8 — 12 and 22.

CHAPTER 8

THE ESSENCE OF CAREER PLANNING

Making the right decision at the right time is always a challenge, but never more so than when the decision concerns your own career. At every stage of your professional life, you need a clear view of your goals, an honest appraisal of your personal strengths and weaknesses, and the courage to adopt a complete change of course, if the situation demands it.

YOUTH, AGE AND OPPORTUNITIES

Today, career track planning and professional development are often systematically handled by employers. Through regular job rotation, major corporations in particular try to confront their young talents with the greatest possible range of challenges. Mindful of Peter Drucker's thoughts on making best use of career opportunities as they arise, this phase of testing the water and frequent change offers an outstanding opportunity to discover where your strengths lie, identify your preferred work methods, review your values, and get a clear view of your primary objectives. Remember, even highly qualified young executives cannot depend on absolute job security. The corporate restructuring measures of recent years have invariably involved job losses—and there is no sign of that changing. In such situations, no qualifications, however good, can stop you losing your job.

But when the dust has settled, the managers who have 'survived' the turmoil can safely assume that it was not just a question of being one of the lucky few, but that there were also qualitative reasons for their survival.

RESPONDING FLEXIBILITY TO CHANGE

Increasingly, the decisive factor is the 'employability' of each individual; their openness and flexibility when faced with change, and their initiative in acquiring skills or experience where these are lacking. The 'survivors' will likely be the career activists who see their careers as projects and themselves as the project managers. The starting point for successful career management is the greatest possible self-knowledge. However, since a fundamental review of your strengths and weaknesses leading to a balanced awareness of both sides is essential, it does not mean that these can be changed or moderated at will, or that they necessarily offset one another. When a person emerges from the formative processes of education and early career, he or she will have a firmly molded personality that, whilst it can be modified or embellished, will retain its core characteristics. As such, it is all the more important to make an honest appraisal of your personality from the outset, and to consider the type of professional environment that would best suit you. Some executives have no taste for the exposure and loneliness of the sole decision-maker and instead prefer to hedge their bets by involving others in the decision process. They feel most at home in an ordered environment, such as they will likely find in a bigger company. Moreover, there are the corporate leaders who thrive best in the clearly structured but unpredictable environment of a smaller company. Perhaps inevitably, many managers kick off their careers in companies that are a poor match for their strengths and weaknesses. Here, resolution and perseverance are called for, as well as the ability to draw one's conclusions and change course when the opportunity arises. Initially, however, every manager should try to attain the maximum in the given setting. An absolute will to give everything your best shot is the decisive criterion in building a successful career. Exceptional performance is the best guarantee that you will be noticed for the right reasons, and that you will find a mentor to support your personal development.

If, however, it becomes clear that you cannot play to your strengths within a specific company, then the time has come to make a change. The ability to make a well-considered change of direction is a key instrument in the career-planning toolbox. It speaks of the kind of energy that can only be an asset for a manager. It is a hallmark of every outstanding executive that they apply their strategic skills not only to corporate policymaking but also in respect of their own personal objectives. Equally, those who are content in their current positions should take care not to lose sight of their own personal goals. If you are going to optimize your career track, you need to be aware at all times of what you want and where you want to be heading. In this way, you will not fail to notice when the time comes for a change of direction. This also implies that a career can embrace several different professions, and indeed such 'patchwork' careers that demand great personal flexibility are becoming more and more common.

EXPERTISE CAREER

Decisions about your career have to be made not only at watershed moments in your biography, but all the time. This said, we have noticed an increasing pattern of career changes occurring when the first half of a professional lifetime draws to a close. The reason is not so much exhaustion as boredom.

Fifteen to twenty years down the career track, the learning curve gradually hits a plateau. The job is less of a challenge and more of a routine.

The degree of job satisfaction falls off and a long bleak road still lies ahead.

OPTIONS AT THE TURNING POINT

At this point, there are various change options open to an executive. Firstly, they can bid farewell to their past career track and enter virgin territory, perhaps in the context of a move into self-employment. A clear-cut change can lead to an immense increase in the value of the individual's acquired potential, such as when an investment banker joins the management team of a private equity firm or a hedge fund, for example. Secondly, they can retain their previous management role, at the same time develop a complementary, parallel career by accepting a directorship of another company, such as a university teaching post for example. A third option is to become a 'social entrepreneur' in a not-for-profit role and to scale down the number of hours dedicated to the 'main' job. Top managers often feel a need later in their careers to look beyond personal gain and give something back to society in a pro bono role. However, irrespective of which of these options leads to a second career, the important thing is to begin preparing for it as early as possible, and then put out feelers in the direction of the desired activity. Adopting alternative roles in the second half of life is not only a way of increasing job satisfaction but can also provide some security against setbacks in one's 'original' career.

AVOIDING THE BLACK HOLE

Despite even the best laid plans, any career can be caught in a blind alley. At an advanced age, when the number of alternatives automatically begins to shrink, such situations can be critical. It is not only in the early stages of a career but also towards the end that a clear and realistic view of one's own perspectives is essential. For those who are willing to accept that they have reached the last stop on their career track, without perhaps achieving everything they set out to do originally, there is still no need to begin to shut down systems and for all performance to fade: if you instead focus on all the positive and constructive aspects of your personality and concentrate on exploiting your rich fund of experience, you can derive great satisfaction from managing this final career segment more effectively.

Such a positive approach has an even greater chance of success if accompanied by the opening up of other perhaps non-professional environments. The discovery of new or long-buried interests in private life can help take a more objective view of professional life. When someone finds that, outside their normal profession, they have a valuable and valued contribution to make, they will have a more relaxed and productive approach to work than those who withdraw into themselves. Opening up such sources of meaning and energy is also the best way of managing a post-retirement life. Many managers experience retirement as a black hole; few confront the prospect head-on and many embrace denial. Furthermore, the vast majority turn their attention to the post-retirement phase far too late. Many underestimate the extent to which they have become addicted to a sense of their own importance in both professional and private life. However, upon retirement, managers are also confronted with the banal normality of everyday life. Few are so popular or in demand that they can prolong their active roles by taking up directorships or travel the world as highly paid public speakers. Dealing with the dark phenomenon of surrendering power calls for maturity and creativity. The imponderables of career planning are at their most pronounced in the early professional years and again towards the end; whilst the latter imponderables may be very different, they are no less challenging. The challenge is to know yourself and to demonstrate courage and continuity because, just as it is dangerous to embark on a career without a plan, a will to learn and the firm intention to give of your best, it is no less hazardous to slip passively into unplanned retirement.

Article by A. Daniel Meiland, Ex CEO&Chairman, Egon Zehnder. First published in Egon Zehnder's magazine Focus in 2001

CHAPTER 9

YOUR PERSONAL BRAND

Personal branding is a process by which we market ourselves to others. A personal brand is not a 'cut and paste' of the profile you write at the top of your CV; a personal brand is about other people's perception of you—and by 'other people' we mean everybody who has a direct or indirect influence on your career. Your personal brand statement should ideally be a compelling two-liner with your competencies.

It is not our objective to write a long and technical chapter about personal branding. If you Google 'How to build my personal brand', you will get all the technical information that you need. Our objective is to explain why it is important to have a personal brand.

You do not get and retain a top executive position without consciously, or unconsciously having built a personal brand. Employers and their recruitment consultants would probably not have found you, if you did not have a very distinct brand, which matches their job specifications. Recruitment of top executives is more and more carried out very professionally with the help of executive search firms. The recruitment is based on very detailed specifications of the job, the skills needed, past achievements, personal characteristics and management style.

Your personal brand is your biggest asset. It is the essence of your reputation, and therefore must be developed and nurtured with great care. One big professional mistake or failure can ruin your brand overnight. Over time, a series of great professional achievements will make your brand stand out from the crowd in the space in which you have decided to excel. By standing out, internal and external recruiters will notice you and understand what your next career move should be.

In this chapter, we suggest that you draft the personal brand you would like to have in the market. But, importantly: do not publish it and do not brag about it. Once you have drafted the personal brand that you would like to have, keep it in a secret place just for yourself.

As you will discover when you read books about 'How to build my personal brand', there are a number of elements that collectively shape your brand, including:

1. Achievements
2. Industry experience and recognition
3. Functional experiences
4. Skill set
5. Personal characteristics
6. Values
7. Dress/personal appearance
8. Hobbies
9. Mobility
10. Family situation

PITFALLS TO BE AWARE OF:

MEDIA: Most people feel flattered when approached by the media. However, we recommend that you do not overexpose yourself and that you only engage with the media on subjects that are strictly relevant to your business. Talk about your company, not about yourself. Once you start talking with the media, it is tempting to go beyond the purely professional matters. Don't do it.

CELEBRITY STATUS: Avoid falling into this trap. Be careful with 'manager of the year awards', etc.

SOCIAL MEDIA: Keep the use of social media strictly professional and never allow anybody else to post on your behalf. Never post late at night and never post inappropriate comments that could damage your personal brand. Remember that the largest and most popular social media channels often retain copyright of your postings, and they store them permanently. It might be fun now, but what will it look like in 20 years' time?

THINGS YOU CAN DO TO INCREASE AWARENESS ABOUT YOUR BRAND:

ARTICLES: Write articles for industry magazines.

PRESENTATIONS: Make presentations at industry forums.

CONFERENCES: Be selective about which ones you attend.

NETWORKING: Industry-specific forums and professional organizations can be a great way of boosting your profile.

CV: Include a very short personal profile that reflects the key features of your professional brand.

SEARCH CONSULTANTS: Creating a long lasting partnership with a search consultant as we describe in Chapter 10 is most likely going to be 'career enhancing'.

In summary, our advise is that you strive to develop a personal brand, which communicates your competencies. In the early part of your career, you should not include a personal brand statement in your CV. Keep it to yourself and you make sure that everything you do throughout your private and professional life safeguards your most important asset. Once you get to the level where you compete for the top job or when you start your second career, it may be time to add your personal brand statement to your CV.

CHAPTER 10

HOW TO WORK WITH EXECUTIVE SEARCH FIRMS

This objective of this chapter is to convey valuable insights to future CEOs that are not readily available in the market. We will help you understand how executive search firms work and how you can significantly enhance your career prospects by establishing a long-lasting partnership with one of the top five global executive search firms, if you dream about becoming a global CEO. These leading companies specialize in serving their clients by recruiting high-calibre executives from about 35-year-old up-and-coming talents.

Aside from the top five global recruiters, there are thousands of large and small employment agencies—both local and regional. These can function admirably for their niche; however, if you want a global career, you should try to build a relationship with one of the top five global search firms.

First, it is important that you understand that the top five firms work for their clients and are paid by their clients. They are not in the business of placing candidates. However, they need to know quality candidates that they can propose to their clients or from whom they can obtain information about the industries in which they work and about potential candidates for specific assignments.

When a young executive begins to be noticed in his or her industry or function, he or she is likely to receiving calls from search firms with an opening phrase that often goes like this: "My name is John, I am a consultant in Search Firm X. Can you talk? ... We have an assignment from one of our clients in your industry and we are looking for the best candidates in the industry for a position as ... Do you happen to know anybody?" Your first thought could well be that you are getting a job offer; however, this is rarely the case.

The best you can envisage is that you might be one of several potential candidates. Nevertheless, the consultant has a much broader agenda: he or she is contacting you believing that you have valuable knowledge about the industry and that you are in a position to help with names of relevant candidates. This approach shows that search firms do not only rely on candidates already in their files. Search consultants do not only call you; they make as many calls as it takes to identify the pool of candidates they need. If you react positively to the call and are helpful, it is very likely that you will receive more calls from the consultant. This may well give you a valuable opportunity to start forming a very important and life-long relationship with the consultant of the search firm.

If you have not been approached by one of the top-five search firms by the time you are about 35 years old but have made a name for yourself in your company, industry or in your function, you should be proactive. Conduct some research to establish which search consultants from which firms you should are relevant for you. The search firms are organized in practices that cover industries and functions. Ask very discreetly around in your industry to identify the most relevant consultants. When it comes to making contact with your chosen consultant(s), you must be completely prepared. If possible, you should try to be introduced to the consultant by someone already well known to him or her.

In the following section, we will detail everything you need to know about building a long-lasting relationship that can pay handsome dividends to both you and the consultant. As with any partnership, it will only work if it is beneficial for both parties.

The benefit to the search firm of working with you is that you will help them do a good job for their clients and that you are likely to become a client yourself, when you rise to a senior executive position. The benefit to you is that you will be assisted and guided through your entire executive career, and you might be considered a candidate for executive and non-executive positions, when you are ready for this.

A BUILDING RELATIONSHIP WITH EXECUTIVE SEARCH FIRMS

1. Try to identify the most relevant consultant at the search firm you want to get in touch with (most have consultant profiles on the internet) based on your specific industry, functional expertise or similarity in backgrounds (e.g. business school)
2. Even better, try and find someone who can introduce you
3. Approach the head-hunter in the industry or functional sector where you have proven expertise
4. Take a long-term perspective on the relationship; it is likely to last for many years
5. See it as a two-way street
6. Stay in touch periodically (every 6 — 12 months)

The executive search profession is relatively young. It was started in the US about 1960. There are now many firms operating in different ways, although there are three main areas of activity. One is leadership search where search firms help companies find better people to meet their objectives. The second is a family of services known as leadership strategic services, where companies want help to evaluate their teams. The final area is board consulting, which is all about proper governance, helping to improve the effectiveness of boards, and helping companies recruit better directors and non-executive directors.

HOW A SEARCH WORKS

Search firms spend time with their clients to understand what they want. Commonly, this is a lengthy process because the client might not grasp entirely what they want. The search firm performs quite a lot of research to identify the type of companies in which suitable candidates might be found and also to identify the people in those companies who would be suitable candidates. This is a desk research phase, which is followed by an active research phase where contact is made with people and recommendations for potential candidates are sought from industry sources. The search firm will talk to people who may have worked with top-level candidates previously to seek references. Of course they also talk with the candidates themselves to discuss the opportunity and to see to whether they're interested.

The next step is a short list of candidates. The best of these are interviewed and the very best are presented to the client with a view to taking them on board.

How do executive search firms work? First, they work for clients and not for job seekers. However, executive search firms are always interested in developing relationships with people early in their career because they are going to be the CEOs of the future. Because people in their pre-CEO careers are future clients, search firms are interested in helping and offering advise. However, you must bear in mind that, as you do not pay them, they do not work for you.

Most consultants will usually work with a number of projects in parallel; usually, this number is between five and ten.

When you are a candidate in a search, you should expect to get a response—even if the search firm does not expect to present you to the client. However, you should not take it personally if it is a generic response, such as, "we will let you know within the next three or four weeks."

Search firms are very interested in engaging with people who are interested in managing their careers, and they help you gain insights and add value. This is often the start of a relationship that will stretch forward to the time that you become a senior manager and to the time that you become a CEO and a client of the search firm.

Whilst you can usually rely on confidentiality, it is also important to be careful. All of the premium branded firms are very confidential in the way they operate, but this is not always the case with some of the smaller players—particularly some of the local players who have often been known to try to sell people to the highest bidder. Therefore, it is important that you try to build a relationship with an executive search consultant whom you can get on with, somebody who knows your industry sector, somebody who can give you useful advise. Take a long-term perspective on the relationship. It may be that nothing happens for a while, but it is useful because you engage with an individual, you are in the confidential database. The consultant will come back to you. It is a two-way street because search firms can get a lot of value from developing relationships with high potential executives.

⬛ SOME PITFALLS WE OBSERVE IN JOB SEEKERS

1. Insufficient preparation to understand a client organization
2. Not asking challenging and insightful questions
3. Being pompous and unpleasant
4. Not being flexible enough in terms of role/responsibility/compensation package
5. Worrying too much about past lay-offs or a career mistake (though these should be in moderation)
6. Assumption that a 'double-switch' is easy

Amongst the pitfalls, we observe are jobseekers not properly prepared for the interviews. The client will easily spot this. If you come to the interview and you do not even know a great deal about the company, the interviewer will also spot it quickly, and it will count significantly against you. It is important to ask challenging and insightful questions, probe what the company is about, probe what the brand means, probe what they are doing in China and in Asia.

Do not worry too much about past lay-offs. If you have had periods in your career where you have not been employed, do not get concerned about it. There are many reasons these days why people take breaks in their career, so you do not need to obsess over this.

Never assume that a double switch is easy, i.e. where you switch industry sectors and switch jobs. In any situation like this, you are going to have to deal with a lot of learning curves simultaneously, which increases the amount of risk you will be under. It requires a great amount of mental ability and a great deal of hard work and not everybody is successful at it. Never assume that a double switch is easy. Try to avoid it and instead make sure that you have a bridge to the next role and then it is more likely to be successful and more likely to progress on your way to becoming a CEO.

⊂ INTERVIEW WITH AN EXECUTIVE SEARCH FIRM

Your CV, if you like, is an elevator speech about you — and it is important that it is very succinct. One record-breaker ran to some 48 pages! CVs on video clips should be avoided. They are inconvenient and take up too much space in databases. Two succinct pages is sufficient, and if you cannot describe what you have done in two pages, you should go back and try again.

1. 1 — 2 pages chronological style. Make it easy to scan in 30 seconds
2. Outline challenges and quantify your achievements
3. Be clear about your responsibilities (people, budget, P&L, geographical scope)
4. Never, ever lie on your CV

When you interview with an executive research firm, the most important thing to do in any interview is not to talk but to listen. Understand, with the search firm, what the job is about. Moreover, be ready to talk conceptually about your career; why your career moves make sense. Also, it is important to provide examples because, often when interviewing people, we're looking for examples of what they have actually achieved and how they've done it. Given the fact that the time for interview is limited, you need to be ready with such types of example.

Do not be frightened to talk about your successes: it's relevant to explain what they are and there's no reason to be shy. You should also talk about areas where you have not been successful and what you have

1. Be ready to talk about your whole career — what is the common theme and story?
2. Some questions are best answered with specific examples; have these ready done about it because that is very interesting. Be transparent as well

3. Communicate successes and be open about failures and development areas
4. Be transparent

D INTERVIEW WITH CLIENT

When you get in front of a client again, it is critically important to listen. The most hollow feedback we get from clients is that the candidate 'was talking all the time' and trying to sell himself too strongly. Never put yourself in that sort of situation.

It is always very important to prepare and to ask very good questions—probing questions. This demonstrates your interest in the opportunity and your interest in the company.

1. Always come prepared and conduct due diligence
2. Remember to listen and to ask good questions. Check back afterwards with your interviewer
3. Do not brag. Strike the right balance between success and learning

E TEST AND REFERENCES

Many employers use psychometric testing. These tests can be important ancillary tools but are not the 'be all and the end all'. Search firms also use reference-taking a lot, so when you give the names of references, you should give the names of people who know you well and who can talk authoritatively about what you have actually achieved.

1. Testing is a good complementary tool but should never replace references
2. A good executive search consultant is thorough and obtains references — informal and formal
3. References are about seniority or friendship but should come from people you have worked with

Working closely with search firms throughout your career can be immensely rewarding for both yourself and the company involved. Ideally, the relationship will evolve as follows:

1. You receive career advise and you help the search firm to understand your industry
2. You become a candidate, and you may be placed into a dream job one, two or three times during your career
3. When you move into a senior executive role you may become a client of the search firm
4. Towards the end of a successful executive career, you will most certainly become a candidate for non-executive board positions because the search firm knows your strengths and weaknesses well
5. The crucial role that a good relationship with a search firm can play at key junctures of your career explains why working with one is so very important

CHAPTER 11

HOW TO PLAN
YOUR CEO CAREER

The purpose of this chapter is to enable you to plan and develop your career. By carefully proceeding through each individual step and figure, you should be able to devise a realistic career plan.

CAREER DEVELOPMENT `FIGURE 1`

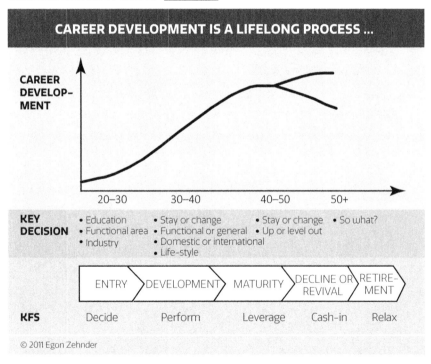

Career development is a lifelong development. Successful CEOs never stop learning and developing their skills.

A generation ago, career planning was not a common thing. Most successful senior leaders would say that their career 'just happened' or that they just got lucky. In today's competitive world, however, where bright graduates compete for the best jobs and where great companies compete for the best talent, it makes a lot of sense to make a proper career plan.

Developing a career is a very important management task with three key elements: firstly, you must have a dream or a vision about what kind of job you would like to have at the peak of your career; secondly, you must have a plan mapping out how you get there; and thirdly, you must execute this plan.

You must be the CEO of your own destiny. This is a task that needs to be executed with a gentle approach, i.e. more 'art' than 'science'. No spreadsheets, no theoretical models, and no bell curves. Planning a career is not an Excel exercise! You must create an *exciting dream* ('vision', in CEO language), and you must plan the journey that you want to embarque on ('execution', in CEO language).

There will be a strong link between how your career develops and how your family life is. It is therefore crucial that your partner is totally involved in defining what kind of dream job you are aiming for and what kind of private life this will give you and your family.

You cannot plan your career in every detail. However, your dream must be turned into a road map, which sets out your goal and the direction you are going to take. As a background for drafting your career plan, we suggest that you take a close look at Figures 1 — 10 in this chapter.

As already mentioned and shown in Figure 1, career development is really a lifelong process. 'Retirement' *per se* no longer exists. In actuality, these days you see more and more top executives re-inventing themselves when their executive career ends.

From time to time, you should ask yourself: Am I in the right place or should I be somewhere else? Career progression is really all about learning from the time that you start your pre-CEO career, move into general management and eventually get your first CEO job.

At all stages, the best advise is that you continuously get new challenges because that is the only way you will really progress on the route to becoming a CEO.

Your long-term potential is driven by a number of factors as you will see in Figure 2.

AMBITIONS, LEADERSHIP COMPETENCIES AND
LEARNING ABILITY FIGURE 2

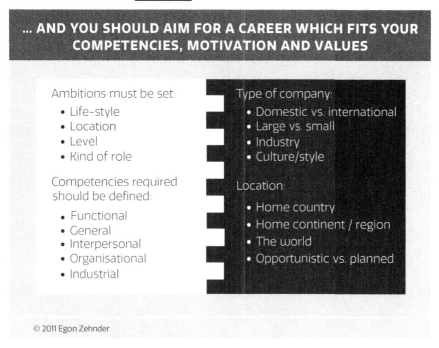

... AND YOU SHOULD AIM FOR A CAREER WHICH FITS YOUR COMPETENCIES, MOTIVATION AND VALUES

Ambitions must be set:
- Life-style
- Location
- Level
- Kind of role

Competencies required should be defined:
- Functional
- General
- Interpersonal
- Organisational
- Industrial

Type of company:
- Domestic vs. international
- Large vs. small
- Industry
- Culture/style

Location:
- Home country
- Home continent / region
- The world
- Opportunistic vs. planned

© 2011 Egon Zehnder

The complexity of the above figure illustrates very clearly that there are many factors to be considered when you plan your career. You need to think very carefully about each of the factors: make the right decisions and stick to them.

AMBITIONS, LEADERSHIP COMPETENCIES AND
LEARNING ABILITY **FIGURE 3**

THREE IMPORTANT ASPECTS
OF YOUR AMBITIONS TOWARDS YOUR DREAM JOB

AMBITION IS CRITICAL: The very fact that you embarked on an MBA and are now reading this book shows that you're pretty ambitious. People have to make quite a lot of sacrifices in order to study to gain an MBA, and ambition is the driving force behind this. You must have ambitions if you want to be successful in business. But you should not only have personal ambitions. To move up the career ladder, your ambitions must include ambitions for your team, for your business unit and very importantly for the company that you work for. When discussing your ambitions with your boss, you should not only ask the question: 'What can the company do for me?' You should also ask the question: 'What can I do for the company?'

LEADERSHIP COMPETENCIES: These are behaviors and capabilities that you develop during the course of your career by being in leadership situations. In order to progress to become a CEO, you need enormous learning ability, which is something that is quite different from ability to learn from books. The critical difference is the ability to take on-board from a whole variety of inputs. We're talking about the ability to ask the right questions; we're talking also about the ability to be very mentally agile, to switch from one subject to the next, to realize when there are certain areas that may no longer be relevant to what you're doing and to move on to new challenges and new ideas.

LEARNING ABILITY: You must have the ability and curiosity to keep learning during your entire career and life. To be a leader means that you must always strive to be ahead.

© 2011 Egon Zehnder

In order to assess your long-time potential to being a CEO, it is worthwhile to pause for reflection from time to time and ask your-self: Am I learning enough? Am I really interested in becoming a CEO? Becoming a CEO has to be something that you want. It may be that you are grandmother has always told you that you are destined to become a CEO and that your friends think you would make a good CEO, but unless *you* actually want to become a CEO and have the ambition to do so, it is not going to happen.

AMBITION, OUR PROFESSIONAL PLATFORM, PERSONALITY AND LIFESTYLE DREATE YOUR PERSONAL BRAND FIGURE 4

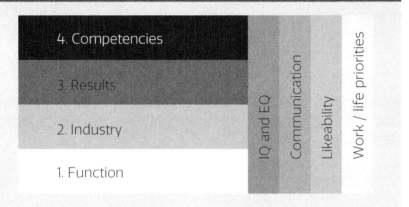

1. Your functional knowledge, which you keep adding to throughout your career. An MBA course is a part of this, as is your initial career development. These need to be maintained and developed continuously.

2. Your industry experience. What sort of industry do you work in? There you should make logical choices that add to your existing competencies.

3. Results are clearly very important because, essentially, that's the way in which you'll be evaluated on your ability to score goals. So it's important that you achieve significant results and typically results ahead of expectations.

4. Competencies, namely critical building blocks, things such as strategic orientation areas, like collaborating and influencing skills, which are very important characteristics and which have important behaviours associated with them, which will take you further forward in your career.

Over time, there is the need to develop a personal brand (Chapter 9) that is essentially, what you are. It is what you have on offer—and that's not only a combination of the four pillars mentioned in Figure 4: It entails a lot of other factors, some of which are relatively 'hard' like IQ and others which are relatively 'soft', i.e. your self-awareness, the way in which you communicate, the extent to which people appreciate you, your likeability. In addition, your work/life priorities are important. For many executives, it is becoming less and less common to make a distinction between work and life; doing so suggests that work is something that is bad and that life is something good, so increasingly we talk about work—life integration, which makes a lot more sense for those of us who actually enjoy what we do.

SIX PIECES OF SOUND ADVISE TO TAKE INTO ACCOUNT WHEN PLANNING YOUR CAREER FIGURE 5

1. Make your career dream a journey rather than a destination.

2. Think about how you create personal brand and what it should stand for

3. Your dream must be realistic. Do not aim for a Forbes 500 CEO job if you're not certain this is right for you. Aim for one of the hundreds of thousands wonderful CEO jobs that you find in both small, medium and large companies

4. Your dream must not become an obsession. This will be noticed by your colleagues and make corporate life intolerable for you and for your colleagues. Worse still, it could defy the objective

5. Do not make a career plan where you fail if you do not quite make it all the way. Being a country CEO is often a much more fulfilling job than being an EVP at HQ

6. Find a mentor to guide you during your early career

© 2011 Egon Zehnder

Let our six pieces of advise sink in and consider them from start to finish during your entire career.

The list below is another source of inspiration throughout your entire career.

1. Choose a role that plays to your strengths and life values. Reflect on your competencies and values

2. Go for blue chip companies early in your career – if you can. They will show you what 'good looks like'

3. Choose a profession and become accomplished in it. Your professional platform is a key part of your personal brand.

4. Build internal and external networks. A good mentor at the right level is worth gold

5. Make sure you can give priority to company goals rather than personal ones. Hard work, loyalty and commitment are the most rewarded

6. Results are what matters. A good career opportunity is a challenge that allows you to show visible results

7. Work on weak spots and leverage your strengths. Realism about your own competencies counts more than a big ego

8. Go for the challenge, not for the title. A good career move gives you opportunity to prove yourself and show results. Title is less important

9. Be focused and proactive but not pushy. Take stock at regular intervals and try to be in the 'driver's seat'

10. Be realistic. It's better to be a top CFO than a weak CEO.

© 2011 Egon Zehnder

Again, we recommend that you think very carefully about each piece of advise, make the right decisions and stick to them. It is worth remembering that CEO jobs come in many sizes (Figure 7), and that aiming for the group CEO job in a Forbes 500 company is a very high-risk proposition. There are tens of thousands of great CEO jobs to aim for, so it is important to be realistic in your ambitions. Get that small CEO job as early as possible in your career, and then move up the ladder as you mature and demonstrate that you have what it takes to be a successful CEO.

CEO JOBS COME IN MANY SIZES

The CEO title appeared towards the end of the last millennium. Until then typical titles for the top executive were President, Chief Executive, Managing director, General Manager, etc. In addition, local versions such as PDG in France, VD in Sweden, etc.

Initially the CEO title was only used for the top executive of the organization. However, due to its catchy appeal the CEO title has spread as wild fire around the world and now covers jobs of many different sizes. It is not uncommon to come across groups with many CEOs: One Group CEO, several Regional or Divisional CEOs, many country CEOs and even more Opco CEOs.

WHAT COMPANIES SEEK IN HIGH POTENTIAL CANDIDATES
FIGURE 7

CHARACTERISTICS AND SKILLS OF HIGH POTENTIAL CANDIDATES
1. Potential, meaning longer termpotential to progress throughout your career
2. Strategic thinking capability
3. Ability to drive change
4. Ability to execute amd deliver results
5. Ability to win
6. Ability to influence other people

© 2011 Egon Zehnder

With our advise from this chapter and your own experience, you should be able to write a compelling CV to help you find the right first job.

PLAN CAREFULLY FOR YOUR JOB INTERVIEWS

The below pre-interview checklist is intended to help you structure your thoughts when you start planning your journey towards your dream job and have interviews with potential employers.

PLAN CAREFULLY FOR YOUR JOB INTERVIEW THAT SHOULD PUT YOU ON TRACK FOR A CEO CAREER `FIGURE 8`

PRE-INTERVIEW CHECKLIST
Lifestyle:
Location(s)
Level
Kind of role
Competencies required:
Functional
General
Interpersonal
Organizational
Industrial
Type of company:
Domestic or global
Large vs. small
Industry
Culture/style
Location:
Home country
Home continent
The world

© 2016 Waldemar Schmidt

DEFINE YOUR CEO DREAMS

The first step to take when you start planning your career is to define your dream job. A dream of becoming a CEO must never become an obsession. It must always be a dream. A dream, which shall be the guiding star throughout your career. It is our experience that many CEOs who have had long and successful careers have exceeded their initial dreams. Consider these examples when you define your dream job:

EXAMPLES OF HOW A DREAM JOB CAN BE EXPRESSED

"My dream is to get my first CEO job in a global firm before I turn 35 and then grow into bigger CEO jobs till I reach my full potential"

"My dream is to become the CEO of a medium-sized public company in my home country"

"My dream is to become Country CEO of a global company in my home country"

"My dream is to take over my uncle's job as CEO of our family business"

"My dream is to become an entrepreneur and CEO of my own company"

"My dream is to join company X and grow into a top CEO position"

© 2016 Waldemar Schmidt

The examples above are included to illustrate how your dream can be formulated. Again, we advise you not to be unrealistic. It is much better to over-achieve than to under-achieve.

YOUR CAREER PLAN

You have mapped out your pre-CEO career and you have defined your dream job. Now it is time to map out how you can get it.

As mentioned, career planning is not a science. It is an art. It qualitative. Not quantitative. And importantly, remember that it may take up to 20 years of hard work to land your CEO dream job.

A career plan is something you keep for yourself and don not brag about. It is however okay to talk about your career dreams. Once you have stepped on to the career ladder and shown noticeable achievements, it will be very natural to talk with your superiors about your next job and about your dream job at the annual performance reviews. If you are fortunate enough to become part of your company's fast track programme for high-potentials, it will also be natural to let your aspirations become known, when you have demonstrated that you deserve the status. Your career plan should of course be in sync with your company's plan for you.

If you start out early in a blue-chip global companies, it would be very unwise to dream about getting the top CEO job and let everybody know about it. There are far too many uncertainties for such a dream to be realistic. The risk of disappointment is huge and you will probably be seen as arrogant by your colleagues, if you talk about it.

Our experience has shown us that most people with CEO aspirations in fact have consciously or unconsciously laid the foundations of a career plan quite early in their lives. Few of today's successful CEOs have made formal career plans. But with increased competition for top jobs we strongly advise you to make a career plan.

EXAMPLE OF A CAREER PLAN

You can draw up a formal career development plan many ways. To inspire you and to illustrate how a career plan may look, we have used the example of a 25-year-old newly graduated Swedish mechanical engineer, Lars. He has just started his search for a job with CEO potential. He speaks good English and basic German. His girlfriend Monica is a Swedish medical doctor and has recently started her career at Karolinska, the university hospital in Stockholm, Sweden. Both have plans of developing their careers and dreams of working abroad for some years before settling in Sweden. They have discussed how both can develop their careers and agreed that Lars' career will have priority, if they one day have to make a choice. Monica has become inspired by our Career Path Chart and have designed a similar one for her career and has mapped out the path to her dream job. They plan to marry in five years' time and to have a family. They agree that it will be an asset for their future children to have an international education. Lars has drafted his career plan with full support from Monica. It looks as follows:

1— MY DREAM IS to join a publicly listed large or medium sized global Swedish engineering company, where I would get the possibility of having a career that potentially can go all the way to a top job before I am 50 years old. If a top CEO job does not become available when I am ready, I will consider joining a similar company in Sweden or in Germany.

2— TO ACHIEVE MY GOAL, I envisage my career path should be something like this:

THE CEO CAREER PATH CHART: LARS

FUTURE CEOs	PRESENT CEOs	RETIRING CEOs
AGE: 25–29	AGE: 35–60	AGE: 60–70
WORKING HOURS/YEAR: 3,000	WORKING HOURS/YEAR: 3,000	WORKING HOURS/YEAR: 2,000 → 1,500 → 0
YEARS IN JOBS: 10	YEARS IN JOBS: 25	YEARS IN JOBS: 10
KNOW YOUR CUSTOMERS: ☐ Sales ☐ Marketing ☑ Customer service	CEO JOBS: ☑ S – Small ☑ M – Medium	SECOND CAREER: ☑ Chairman role ☑ Board member ☑ Other roles
KNOW YOUR PRODUCTS: ☐ Operations ☑ Manufacturing ☐ Supply chain ☐ Technology	☑ L – Large ☐ XL – Extra large ☐ XXL – Forbes Global 2000 company	THIRD CAREER: ☐ Board roles ☑ Investor ☑ Mentor ☐ Speaker & writer ☑ Pro-bono roles
KNOW YOUR NUMBERS: ☐ Accounting ☑ Business control ☐ Management consultancy (Strategy and operations) ☑ Junior management positions	AN UNEXPECTED EVENT MAKES YOU: ☐ CEO – because you were there as CFO, COO or board member	RETIREMENT: ☐ Pro-bono roles ☑ Investor ☐ Mentor ☐ Other: ☑ No more business roles

3 – ADDITIONAL EDUCATION

I will need to acquire expertise in finance, marketing and general management by attending courses.

4 – POTENTIAL EMPLOYERS

I will apply for jobs in the following companies in Sweden: X,Y,Z...

5 – PLAN B1

If I cannot get a suitable first job with one of my preferred Swedish companies, I will switch my attention to the Swedish subsidiaries of the largest German engineering companies.

6 – PLAN B2

If I don't progress fast enough towards my goal in my first company I will try to move to another Swedish or German engineering company.

The objective of our career plan example is to illustrate what we believe are the most important aspects of a career plan:

A. Be clear about your dream job
B. Be very thorough with your pre-CEO career
C. Have one or more Plan Bs in place
D. Be clear on the work-life implications of an ambitious career

CHAPTER 12

HOW TO PLAN AND EXECUTE YOUR PRE-CEO JOBS

YOUR PRE-CEO CAREER IS YOUR TRANSITION FROM SPECIALIST JOBS TO MANAGEMENT JOBS WITH RESPONSIBILITY FOR PEOPLE AND RESULTS

You have made your self-assessment and come to the conclusion that you are fit and willing to embark on a career that can lead to a CEO position. You have drafted a personal brand statement, drawn up a compelling CV, and formulated a career dream /goal. You have drafted your first career plan and planned how you propose to get there. Now, the critical task is to find the right job to start with. A careful reading of the preceding chapters should enable you to do a good job of getting that crucial first career position. In Chapter 8 and Chapter 11 you can find inspiration regarding the best path to follow for a CEO job. As you can see, there are many ways to go about it.

If you are clear on the industries you like and the ones you do not like, you should identify the companies where you can have a career and achieve your goal. If you are not quite clear on the industry that you would like to work in, we suggest that you plan to start your career in one or two different industries or companies, where you can gain relevant functional experience in two or more different functions.

If you want to pursue the CFO track to a CEO job, you must also try to acquire experience in different functions (accounting, treasury, controlling, etc.) in companies that are recognized as leading-edge in the financial area. As already mentioned we strongly recommend that you gain experience from a sales and marketing function and in supply-chain functions. We believe that a CEO must have an in-depth customer experience and operations experience. You have mapped out your pre-CEO career in Chapter 6:

THE CEO CAREER PATH CHART

FUTURE CEOs	PRESENT CEOs	RETIRING CEOs
AGE: 25–35/40	AGE: 35/40–60/65	AGE: 60/65–70/80
WORKING HOURS/YEAR: 3,000	WORKING HOURS/YEAR: 3,000	WORKING HOURS/YEAR: 2,000 ➔ 1,000 ➔ 0
YEARS IN JOBS: 10–15	YEARS IN JOBS: 20–30	YEARS IN JOBS: 10–20
KNOW YOUR CUSTOMERS: ☐ Sales ☐ Marketing ☐ Customer service	CEO JOBS: ☐ S – Small ☐ M – Medium	SECOND CAREER: ☐ Chairman role ☐ Board member ☐ Other roles
KNOW YOUR PRODUCTS: ☐ Operations ☐ Manufacturing ☐ Supply chain ☐ Technology	☐ L – Large ☐ XL – Extra large ☐ XXL – Forbes Global 2000 company	THIRD CAREER: ☐ Board roles ☐ Investor ☐ Mentor ☐ Speaker & writer ☐ Pro-bono roles
KNOW YOUR NUMBERS: ☐ Accounting ☐ Business control ☐ Management consultancy (Strategy and operations) ☐ Junior management positions	AN UNEXPECTED EVENT MAKES YOU: ☐ CEO – because you were there as CFO, COO or board member	RETIREMENT: ☐ Pro-bono roles ☐ Investor ☐ Mentor ☐ Other: ☐ No more business roles

PLANNING YOUR PRE-CEO CAREER

Your starting point will be the shortlist of industries and the companies you have chosen as relevant to you. In order to prioritise the companies on your list, you should find the answers to a number of questions, such as:

1. What business culture do they have?
2. Will they offer me an international career?
3. Do they have a fast track programme that I can join?
4. Do they have a good track record of employing and developing people like me?
5. How far up the organization, can I possibly get?
6. Do my skills, personality and ambitions fit with the company's requirements?
7. Can I become passionate about their products and services?
8. Is the company slow or fast growing?

Once you have done your homework, i.e. produced a comprehensive list of relevant potential employers, you will need to determine how to approach them. Here are some hints:

1. Large companies tend to be very structured when hiring people like you which means that you must discover their method of graduate recruitment
2. Smaller companies are sometimes less rigid which means that a well-motivated unsolicited approach could work
3. Finding companies with bosses with degrees from your school or university can sometimes open doors
4. Networking is important

Now is the time to be the CEO of your own future. Planning a career and finding a job requires thorough planning and execution as we have described in Chapter 8 and Chapter 11.

In your pre-CEO jobs there are a number of things that you must do:

1. Work internationally
2. Acquire functional experience in areas different from your education
3. Get a job with responsibility for people and P&L as early as you can
4. Gain recognition for your achievements, results, management style and team building capability

The pre-CEO period of your life should be very exciting. There is probably a lot going on in your private life as well: you may marry and have children, move to different countries with your family, absorb new cultures, learn new languages, get bigger and bigger jobs, and much more. This is a period of your life where our advise in Chapter 22 about work-life balance is very important.

However, this period of your life will never be a bed of roses. You will face difficulties and challenges both in your private life and in your professional life. Taking on jobs in unfamiliar functions will be challenging,

This period can go two ways. The first is that you live the dream and with determination ensure that you reach the goal you have set in your career plan and ensure that your family has a fulfilling life.

The second is that everything descends into chaos for yourself and your family because you make poor judgement calls, underperform, fall out with colleagues and superiors, become accident-prone or have family problems.

Tackling problems with a positive attitude will go a long way towards ensuring that your pre-CEO career pans out in the best possible way.

In order to help you navigate during this period we have picked a selection of dilemmas from our 'A—Z CEO career guide', which we think are very relevant for you to look into at this point, of your career planning. We suggest that you reflect on the inspiration given below:

ATTITUDE: Great leaders have a positive attitude.

BUILDING TEAMS: Great leaders understand the importance of having great teams with complementary skills around them. They know how to recruit, develop and retain their team members. They are not afraid of giving people challenging jobs.

MISTAKES: Only people who do nothing avoid making mistakes. When you make mistakes, learn from them and never make the same mistake again. Remember to take the blame, when you or your team has erred. Recognize that you do not become a great leader, if you constantly fear failure.

MAKING AN IMPACT: If you wish to become a CEO, your work must make an impact in the company. Throughout your career, your CV must have new real 'achievements' in each of the jobs that you have had. People who do not make a difference will not become CEOs.

MENTOR: The right mentor (including executive search consultants), especially in your early career, can be worth his or her weight in gold. Get advise when you need to make critical decisions. Listen, but make your own decisions.

NETWORK: Building and maintaining a network of relevant people is very important in your business life as well as in your private life. But remember that a network can only be sustained if it is based on a two-way communication. If you receive, you also have to give.

NICE: It is better for your career to be nice rather than pushy.

PATIENCE: Great leaders and successful CEOs are normally not very patient when it comes to performance. There are times during your career when being patient pays off. If you feel that your next promotion is overdue, you may start looking for opportunities elsewhere. In big organizations, unexpected things happen all the time. Here too patience may pay off.

SACRIFICES: Executives who love what they do and who are in control do not feel that they make sacrifices.

SILOS: Many companies are organized by line of business and some by geography. Lines of business are often called "silos". Moving from one "silo" to another in the same company is often very difficult or even impossible. The same goes for geography: if you spend most of your time in one particular region, you may be stuck there if you do not make a special effort to move on.

UNEXPECTED EVENTS: Be ready for unexpected events. They will occur. See unexpected events as opportunities. If a CEO role suddenly becomes available in a country that is not on your list, go for it. If one of your superiors leave suddenly, do not say no to his or her job because you feel that you are not ready for it. If you can swim, you can also swim in deep waters.

Use our career chart to plan your path to your first CEO job:

THE CEO CAREER PATH CHART		
FUTURE CEOs	**PRESENT CEOs**	**RETIRING CEOs**
AGE: 25–35/40	AGE: 35/40–60/65	AGE: 60/65–70/80
WORKING HOURS/YEAR: 3,000	WORKING HOURS/YEAR: 3,000	WORKING HOURS/YEAR: 2,000 → 1,000 → 0
YEARS IN JOBS: 10–15	YEARS IN JOBS: 20–30	YEARS IN JOBS: 10–20
KNOW YOUR CUSTOMERS: ☐ Sales ☐ Marketing ☐ Customer service	CEO JOBS: ☐ S – Small ☐ M – Medium	SECOND CAREER: ☐ Chairman role ☐ Board member ☐ Other roles
KNOW YOUR PRODUCTS: ☐ Operations ☐ Manufacturing ☐ Supply chain ☐ Technology	☐ L – Large ☐ XL – Extra large ☐ XXL – Forbes Global 2000 company	THIRD CAREER: ☐ Board roles ☐ Investor ☐ Mentor ☐ Speaker & writer ☐ Pro-bono roles
KNOW YOUR NUMBERS: ☐ Accounting ☐ Business control ☐ Management consultancy (Strategy and operations) ☐ Junior management positions	AN UNEXPECTED EVENT MAKES YOU: ☐ CEO – because you were there as CFO, COO or board member	RETIREMENT: ☐ Pro-bono roles ☐ Investor ☐ Mentor ☐ Other: ☐ No more business roles

© 2020 Waldemar Schmidt

CHAPTER 13

HOW TO SUCCEED IN YOUR FIRST CEO JOB

Getting your first CEO job is very special. You have been spotted as someone who can lead people and produce results, or maybe as someone who seems to have the potential to do just that. You probably feel proud, but humble. It is quite normal if you ask yourself the question: "Can I master the CEO job?" You have a new and untested work situation: You have a new superior and report to HQ or maybe a board. You are the CEO of a company or a business unit. You may be in a new country, have responsibility for more people, for financial results, new office, bigger company car, higher salary and bonus, higher risk of losing the job, etc.

From the moment you are appointed to the first CEO job you are in the limelight and will continue to be so as long as you are a CEO. Your team will look to you for leadership. Your superiors will look for results. And the bigger your job the stronger becomes the limelight.

To help you succeed in your first CEO job, we start by describing five common situations, which can lead to your first CEO job:

YOUR FIRST CEO JOB IS IN YOUR EXISTING COMPANY

When you get your first CEO job it should ideally be in the company that you are already working in. It can be as CEO and country manager of a small country, a business unit or similar. You are given the job, because your superiors know your strengths and weaknesses have seen what you are capable of and because they see potential in you. You know the company and its strategy, culture, values, etc. wherefore the risk of failure is smaller than in a new company.

YOUR FIRST CEO JOB IS IN A NEW COMPANY DURING OR AFTER YOUR PRE–CEO CAREER

You may have applied for the job or you may have been headhunted to a new company. For obvious reasons this is a more risky career move than being promoted to a CEO job in your company; and the risk increases dramatically if your move is a so called 'double switch'; i.e. when you move from being a sales and marketing manager in the pharmaceutical industry to becoming CEO of a software company.

YOUR FIRST CEO JOB IN ANOTHER COMPANY AT A MATURE AGE

You pre-CEO career goes on for a very long period while you impatiently keep dreaming of your first CEO job. Your judgement tells you that you will not get your first CEO job CEO job in your present company. You are therefore prepared to take the risk and move elsewhere. You have kept close contact with a search firm as we suggest in Chapter 10 and let them know that you are ready for a suitable CEO position. The search may firm places you in a CEO position, which could be a 'double switch'. You are well aware of the added risk that this means. But you really want to become a CEO and you take the CEO job that you are offered.

YOUR FIRST CEO JOB IN YOUR EXISTING COMPANY LATE IN YOUR CAREER

You are a mature CFO, COO or similar. Your CEO suddenly leaves the company and the board decides to offer you the vacant CEO position. You may not have much time to accept or decline the job and you may even not have dreamt of becoming a top CEO. You will have to make a quick risk analyses as part of your decision-making. If no major strategic change is required, the risk of not succeeding is probably limited, wherefore you should accept the opportunity. If the board wants a new strategy, it may be too risky for you to accept the opportunity. We recommend that you discuss the opportunity with your partner and the likely impact that accepting the CEO job will have on your work-life situation. If you decide to decline the offer, the board may well ask you to be the interim CEO until a new CEO is found. We recommend that you accept the interim position to discover whether you have what it takes to become a successful CEO.

YOUR FIRST CEO JOB IS IN A CLIENT COMPANY WHERE YOU HAVE LEAD A MAJOR STRATEGIG PROJECT

If you as a consultant have lead a major strategic project and have presented a convincing report to your client's board, the board may ask you to become the CEO and implement your proposed strategy. If you believe that you have what it takes to become a successful CEO, you should seriously consider accepting the offer. If you see yourself as an advisor you should not.

PREPARE TAKING ON YOUR FIRST CEO JOB

Whatever circumstances lie behind the promotion to your first CEO job, you must carefully plan for this exiting and critical career move. To help you tackle the move to your first CEO position, we have listed a number of subjects for you to consider:

CONTRACT, JOB DESCRIPTION AND SOP: Management of expectations is an important CEO task. It is extremely important that there is absolute clarity regarding the company's *expectations* to your performance. What does the company expect from you during your tenure? What are your success criteria? Whom do you report to? Is there a matrix organization where you will have several superiors? What should your contribution to the Group's results and strategy be?

You therefore need a very serious conversation with your new boss to agree to your contract, a job description, a budget and a SOP-STANDARD OF Performance with 3-5 financial KPIs and 3—5 non-financial KPIs.

If your first CEO job is with your existing company it should not require a lot of negotiation to agree a contract. Do not negotiate too hard and do not bring in your lawyer. Getting your first CEO job is so important for the rest of your career and your life that the salary should not be an obstacle. Your employment contract in this case may be an employment letter. The length of the term is probably about 2—4 years. Your incentives should be linked to the KPIs in your SOP.

If your first CEO job is with a new company, where the risk of failure is higher, you may negotiate a little harder, consult with your lawyer and get a proper management contract.

BE YOURSELF: Whatever the circumstances and the size of your first CEO job you got it because of who you are. Do not change the way you are and behave, just because you are now a CEO. In particular, make sure that success does not make you arrogant or over-confident. Continue to develop your leadership and management skills.

LISTEN MORE THAN YOU TALK: Great leaders listen and learn by asking great questions and by listening. Keep your pre-meditated opinions for yourself until you know the job really well. The best way to learn about your new job and its strengths & weaknesses and opportunities & threats is to ask great questions and to listen.

GET TO KNOW YOUR TEAM: as part of the hand-over, the out-going CEO should give you his or her evaluation of the team members. Be aware that it is quite common that a team member considered a low performer by the leaving CEO becomes a high performer under a new CEO. Meet as many staff as possible to get to know them, understand what they do, ask them how they see the company and what ideas they have for the strategy of the company.

UNDERSTAND THE COMPANY'S MAIN CHALLENGES: Under-standing the company's daily life, values, historic performance against budgets, adherence and contribution to group strategy, competitive situation, etc. is key for your task ahead.

CUSTOMERS: Meet key customers and get their feedback on the company. If relevant, do the same with key suppliers.

EXPECTATIONS: Share the content of your SOP with your colleagues and make sure that they are with the KPIs that you have agreed with your boss.

STRATEGY: At your first quarterly review with your superior, you should have enough information to review the existing strategy for the business. If no strategy exists, draft a strategy paper for the business together with your team. The format of the strategy document depends on the planning process of your company. If necessary, adopt your SOP accordingly.

You are now the leader and you must remember to work CEO task #1: Developing the strategy with your team! You may just have to introduce minor changes to the existing strategy. If you need major changes you must obtain approval from your superior.

BUILD A STRONG TEAM: Remember CEO task #2: great leaders recruit and develop strong teams. A strong team with a shared vision about what to achieve is a winning formula. You therefore need to judge the team that you take over. As already, mentioned predecessors should give his or her valuation of the team members to the new CEO. As mentioned, it is quite common that a team member seen as a low performer by the leaving CEO becomes a high performer under a new CEO. If you after a certain period conclude that you have a low performing member of your team with no potential to improve, you should not hesitate to make a change. Experience shows that nobody wins by delaying such a decision.

EXECUTION: Remember CEO task #3: Deliver results with your team. CEOs are evaluated on their ability to deliver results year-after year. HOW the results are delivered is very important.

You and your team have to be prepared for unexpected events, which can make it impossible for you to deliver the expected results. If the unexpected happens, you have to show leadership and introduce corrective action together with your team to put the company back on track. If you have a good case, your boss or your board will understand and accept.

YOUR MANAGEMENT STYLE: You have some management experience from your pre-CEO jobs. Climbing the CEO ladder means that you will move further away from 'the floor'. It is therefore important to continue leading as a visible playing coach and not becoming a micro manager behind your desk.

LEARN: Successful CEOs keep learning throughout their careers. Your first CEO job is an opportunity to learn a lot. You have the opportunity to get very practical and necessary on-the-job training in all three key business functions (finance, operations/supply chain and sales/marketing/customer service and HR by spending a serious amount of time in these functions. CEOs learn continuously. As an annual or bi-annual routine, you should consider spending a week at a business school for relevant learning, inspiration and reflection. In addition, you should learn from your superiors and from your colleagues, your costumers and other stakeholders. You may also find that seeking regular inspiration from THE JOB OF THE CEO may continue to inspire you.

WORK–LIFE BALANCE: In Chapter 12 we describe how your work-life balance may look like during your pre-CEO career. The situation will probably not change in your first CEO job. We therefore recommend that you and your partner discuss and agree to how you can find the right balance being effective on your job and being present when at home. If both of you work and if you have moved to a foreign country or continent, it is even more important that you discuss and agree how you will prioritise your work-life balance. From time to time you should formally discuss and adjust if necessary as we recommend in Chapter 22, *How to Manage Your Work-life Balance.*

PREPARE YOUR MOVE TO THE NEXT CEO JOB: If your tenure is agreed to be 2—4 years, you should leave the planning of your move to the next CEO role until you have proven that you deserve a bigger CEO job. And it is important not to talk about your next job with anybody; except your partner. But during your tenure you should understand and think about what matters for you to get a new and bigger CEO job:

SUCCESSION: Without suitable candidates available your next move will be delayed. You must therefore have one or more suitable candidates available before you can move. You are not the one to appoint your successor, but you have the duty and the right to make sure that you have one or more candidates ready.

PERFORMANCE: It goes without saying that you must have met or exceeded the expectations to your performance with the *right* management style.

TIMING: If you do really well, a successor is available and a sudden need for a CEO of a bigger business than yours arise in your group you may be asked to move earlier than planned. Your next move can also be delayed in spite of your performance, in which case we advise you to be patient. You need to be flexible either way.

EXIT: When your move is announced in the company, you should prepare a hand over note to your successor.

THE SECOND CEO JOB: At the annual review, 12 months before your planned exit it would be appropriate that you start talking with your boss about your next move. When you got your first CEO job you were willing to go anywhere in the world. This time around, you know the company much better and it would be appropriate to mention the CEO jobs in the group that you would be most interested in. In your career plan, you have laid out which next CEO job you should ideally have. It is however likely that you have learnt more about the options. You may therefore have to adjust your career plan. If you have met or exceeded to the expectations laid out in your engagement memo, you should be well placed for a career move in your group or with another company. You may even be in the ideal position where several senior executives in your group want you. You could also be in a situation where a relevant CEO job is not available in the division that you work in or in your group. Whatever your situation you must again put all your efforts into getting that second CEO job and not be too demanding regarding pay and location.

IF THE CEO JOB IS NOT FOR YOU: During the period of your first CEO job you may come to the conclusion that a CEO job is not right for you. You may be underperforming; you may find the work-life balance too tough, etc. If you conclude that you have been over promoted and the CEO job is not for you, we recommend that you in a mature manner inform your superior about your decision and the motives behind the decision. This is much better for your career than waiting until your boss tells you that you are not up to the job. Your short CEO experience is however a very valuable lesson for your future career and should help you make a new career plan that plays to your strengths and the work-life balance that you want.

IF YOU HAVE BEEN SUCCESSFUL IN YOUR FIRST CEO JOB: Go to Chapter 14, *How To succeed in Your Next CEO Jobs.*

HOW TO SUCCEED IN YOUR NEXT CEO JOBS

Having successfully completed your first CEO job and moving on to the next CEO jobs are very important achievements.

Taking on the first CEO job feels overwhelming for most people. Almost intimidating. The feeling you get when you move to your next and bigger CEO jobs in your company may be less overwhelming. Your level of confidence has increased with the success of your first CEO job. But you are aware that a bigger CEO job means more attention from everywhere and that you must not be overconfident.

If your second or third CEO job is in a new company, perhaps a new industry, in a new country or continent and perhaps with a different kind of ownership, you have good reasons to feel overwhelmed, as you did when you got your first CEO job.

In any case, as you move up the CEO ladder the scope of your job and its responsibilities increases. You may now report to a formal or an informal board, have increased financial responsibility, be more involved in the group's strategy matters, etc. You therefore have a lot to learn again.

To help you tackle the move to your CEO job number two or three we have in the following summarized our experience concerning a number of key subjects that you will have to deal with. We suggest that you include them in your plan for how you will manage you career move and what you can do to make a success of it. The subjects are the same as the ones we propose for your first CEO job, but our advise is adjusted to the new situation.

TAKING ON YOUR NEXT CEO JOBS

CONTRACT, JOB DESCRIPTION, BUDGET AND CEO: It is extremely important that there is absolute clarity regarding the company's expectations to your performance. *Management of expectations* continue to be a key CEO task. What does the company expect from you during your tenure? What kind of job do they want you to do? Turn-around, cost cutting, profit improvement, restructuring, organic growth, new strategy, new organization, merger, acquisitions, etc? You therefore need a serious conversation with your new superior or chairman, where you agree your contract, a job description, the budget a SOP-STANDARD OF PERFORMANCE with 3—5 financial KPIs and 3—5 non-financial KPIs with your superior.

Before you take on the job, we suggest that you meet all relevant persons to learn about the job to get their perspectives on your new job.

If your next CEO job is with your present company it should not require a lot of negotiation to agree your terms. Do not negotiate too hard. Getting your next CEO jobs is also very important for the rest of your career and your life. The length of the contract is probably about 3—5 years. You may get an employment letter rather than an employment contract, which is fine, as long as all key points are covered. Your incentives should be linked to the KPIs that you have agreed with your boss.

If your next CEO job is with a new company, where the risk of failure is higher, you should negotiate a little harder and get a proper employment contract. If you are a senior executive, this could be a Group CEO job and your final job in which case you need to negotiate accordingly.

BE YOURSELF: Whatever the circumstances and the size of your CEO job you got it because of who you are. Do not change the way you are and behave, just because you are now a CEO of a bigger company. In particular, make sure that success does not make you arrogant and overconfident. However, make sure that you continue to develop as a leader.

If your second or third CEO job is with your present company, you will be familiar with its strategy, culture, values, un-written rules, products and many of its people. If your second or third CEO job is in a new company, you will have a very steep learning curve ahead of you to fully understand your new company.

Be aware that everybody in your new company will watch you and will be anxious to know which changes you may want to introduce to the strategy and their jobs.

LISTEN MORE THAN YOU TALK: Great leaders learn by asking great questions and by listening. The best way to learn about your new company, its strengths and weaknesses, opportunities and threats is to ask questions and to listen. We therefore suggest that you ask many relevant questions and keep any premeditated opinions that you may have to yourself, until you know the company's situation really well.

UNDERSTAND THE COMPANY'S MAIN CHALLENGES: Learn about the company's main challenges and its past performance against budgets, last year, group strategy, competition, employee satisfaction, customer satisfaction, etc. Understanding the company's daily life, values, historic performance against budgets, adherence and contribution to group strategy, competitive situation, etc. is key for your task ahead.

CUSTOMERS: Meet key customers and get their feedback on the company. If relevant, do the same with key suppliers.

EXPECTATIONS: Share the content of your SOP with your management team and make sure that they get aligned with the KPIs that you have agreed with your boss.

PREPARE A PLAN STRATEGY WITH YOUR TEAM: As CEO in a bigger job you will be more involved in formulation of the strategy. We therefore suggest that you prepare a proper strategy plan together with your team. You should either revise the existing strategy or create a new one. The strategy must take the scope of your job and the group strategy into account.

PRESENTATION OF STRATEGY: At your first business review meeting (or board meeting) it is time to present the strategy plan that you have prepared together with your team. The format of the strategy documents depends on the kind of company that you are the CEO of.

EXECUTION: Let us start with some very important advise for new CEOs as well as seasoned CEOs: Remember CEO task #3: Deliver results with your team. CEOs are evaluated on their ability to deliver results year-after-year. Remember that a CEO's success is both on WHAT he or she delivers and on HOW he or she delivers the results. This last part sometimes come to the fore, when a CEO, who has consistently delivered, is dismissed because the board did not like the way he or she delivered the results.

There will be times where the unexpected happens and you therefore cannot deliver the agreed results. When that is the case you have to show leadership and introduce corrective action that will put the company back on track. If you have a good case, your boss or your board will understand and accept. Great leaders do not give their bosses 'profit warnings' without having a plan with corrective action.

BUILD A STRONG TEAM: Remember CEO task #2: Great leaders recruit and develop strong teams. A strong team with a shared vision about what they want to achieve is a winning formula. As already mentioned you may not always agree with your predecessor about the quality of all team members. You therefore need to judge the team that you take over. Strangely enough, it is quite common that a team member seen as a low performer by the leaving CEO becomes a high performer under a new CEO. If you after a certain period conclude that you have a low performing member of your team with no potential to improve, you should not hesitate to make a change. Experience shows that nobody wins by delaying the decision.

YOUR MANAGEMENT STYLE: Let us remind you that one of the reasons that you got the new CEO job was because of who you are and your management style. You should therefore not change the basics, but you have to continue to develop to become an even better leader. Sticking to the concept of playing coach will continue to be effective and appreciated by your team. Your management style is an important part of your appraisal.

LEARN: Great leaders continue to learn throughout their careers. Whether your second or third CEO job is in your old company or in a new company there is a lot to learn. In order to keep learning and improving your management and leadership skills, we recommend that you attend relevant courses at top business school from time to time. Attending such courses is also an opportunity to reflect and learn from the peers that you meet outside the lecture room. You may also find that THE JOB OF THE CEO may continue to inspire you.

STAY IN CEO JOB #2 OR MOVE ON: You may find that CEO job #2 is your dream job and you therefore would like to stay in it until your retirement. Such a situation could well occur if you are the CEO of a S, or L company or group with untapped potential in which you can continue to grow. You may now want to go to Chapter 15 for some useful advise.

You may discover that your second CEO is your dream job and therefore want to remain in the job until you retire. Your second CEO job could be in a S- or M-sized company or group with potential for further development. If your horizon is 10 or more years in the job, it is essential that you remain a great leader full of initiatives and energy.

PREPARE THE MOVE TO YOUR DREAM CEO JOB: You must leave the planning of the move to your dream job until you have proven that you deserve to be considered a suitable candidate for the top job until all conditions are in place. This is true whether your dream job is in your present company or whether it is in a new company. The move is going to be very challenging. Among things to consider are:

PERFORMANCE: Your performance during your career till now must have met or exceeded expectations in terms of results, management style, team building, etc. Go to Chapter 21 for further advise.

SUCCESSION: You must have one or more suitable candidates in place to take over your job.

WORK–LIFE BALANCE: You and your partner must agree that it is still right for you to go for your last CEO job.

If you are a candidate for your dream job in your present company, you should proceed to Chapter 15.

If your dream job is not in your present company, we assume that you have discussed this for a long time with your search consultant and therefore have prepared yourself carefully for this critical career move.

HOW TO SUCCEED IN YOUR LAST CEO JOB

GETTING THE TOP JOB

When you are 45—50 years of age, you should be in the position where you are a strong candidate for your dream CEO job in your company or in another company. However, it is extremely difficult to foresee just when these jobs become available. It would take a lot of luck to get the timing right in your own company. Your boss may stay until the last day of his or her contract or may suddenly leave due to poor performance, health issues or a new job somewhere else. Your chances of getting the top job in your group will also depend on competition from internal and external candidates and on the competencies that are required. Aiming for the top job in your company is a very risky proposition. We therefore recommend that you prepare Plan B.

Competent boards have a succession plan in place and often use executive search firms to help them evaluate both internal and external candidates for the top job. Having got so far, it is very likely that you are one of the internal candidates. If the departure of the group CEO has been on the cards for a while, it is also very likely that internal candidates in various ways have played political games to position themselves for the top job. The internal competition in these situations is often so fierce that the 'losers' leave the company if they do not get the top job.

To be a strong candidate for a top CEO job, you will be well-advised to stay out of the political game. What counts is that you are able to clearly and convincingly demonstrate that you have the following traits:

1. A long track record with several CEO positions successfully managing a large country, a region or division and having consistently delivered great results and healthy growth with a positive management style
2. Worked in different countries and continents
3. Successfully managed businesses through all kinds of business cycles, carried out change programs and integrated acquired businesses
4. A deep understanding of your business and industry
5. Recruited, developed and retained outstanding teams and have a very credible succession plan in place for your part of the group
6. Positively contributed to developing and executing the strategy of your group

In our experience, boards commonly choose an internal candidate if the company is performing well with no need for a major strategic overhaul. The CFO is an obvious and often strong candidate in such a situation. The board knows the CFO and sees him or her as a safe pair of hands.

If major changes are necessary, many boards will appoint an external candidate. Knowing whether major changes are necessary by the board should give you an indication of your chances for getting the top job.

Whoever is appointed, is chosen because of his or her achievements and talents. If you get the top job our advise is that you remain your natural self—the person the board appointed. There is no need to change your personality or modify your modus operandi just because you become group CEO. Remember that your extensive knowledge of the company in which you have advanced through the ranks and acquired a strong grasp of key functional areas equips you admirably for the post of Group CEO.

If you get the top CEO job, you will feel the responsibility. Everybody looks to you for leadership. Your old colleagues, the board and everybody else recognizes that you are the number one with the final say in all important matters.

We assume that you will consider your new CEO job as your final job and that you therefore can negotiate the terms and conditions without drama.

STRATEGY, BUDGETS, JOB DESCRIPTION AND CONTRACT: Management of expectations is now more critical than ever. It is therefore very important that you agree strategy, budgets, job description and your contract with your chairman.

If you do not get the top CEO job in your company, you should go to Chapter 17.

MANAGING YOUR FINAL CEO JOB

You must get on with the new job immediately. As discussed in Chapter 1 about the job of the CEO, it is primarily about creating long-term shareholder value WITH A STAKEHOLDER VALUE CONCEPT.

Remember our simple job description of the CEO role:

1. Develop the strategy with your team and keep it fresh during your tenure
2. Develop and recruit smart people for your team
3. Execute the strategy with your team
4. And let us repeat—do *not* lose focus or get carried away if you are successful. Do not become an arrogant Celebrity CEO. Stay with the personality and style you had when you were appointed to the job. Remember that your *management style* will account for 20% of your appraisal

Your first task will, in all likelihood be to ensure that you have the right team around you. If your peers who did not get the job are not happy and you are not happy, they will have to leave. This in turn creates opportunities for other talents.

Your second important job will be that you and your team examine the strategy to determine whether adjustments are necessary. Investors, analysts and the media seem to believe that a new CEO means a new strategy after 100 days. In well-managed and well-performing companies, there should not be the need for a total review. In any case, in order to inform all internal and external stakeholders about the company's strategy under your leadership, it would be very wise to make an announcement on the subject as early as possible to remove the uncertainty that the appointment of a new CEO always causes.

As part of the process that led to your appointment, you will have given the chairman your thoughts regarding the strategy and the team. When appointing you, the board has agreed and accepted your thoughts about these two important matters. Your first priority in the job is therefore to assemble your team, revisit the strategy with the team, get the board's approval and make an announcement. If your company is a listed company, the time to do so is in the first quarterly report under your reign, i.e. less than 100 days after you took over your dream job.

Once you have the strategy and your team in place, the job is about relentlessly executing the strategy with your team and overcoming roadblocks and unexpected events.

KEEPING THE CEO JOB

You are now in your dream job in a company where you have spent a considerable time of your career.

Remember our quote:

> *"It is very difficult to get a CEO job.*
> *But it is even more difficult to keep it."*

To help you keeping your new job we have prepared a list below with advise gathered through many years of experience. There is however no simple method to secure that you will be successful in your new job over a very long period. But we believe that our list can help you stay in your final CEO job, as long as you would like. There are many things that you need to be aware of. We have tried to focus on the essential ones to help you:

1. Remind yourself from time to time that: '80% of a CEOs success is WHAT is delivered and 20% is about HOW it is delivered'. Staying close to your chairman, the board, investors, your key stakeholders and your team should help you understand how other people think you are performing on both parameters. Maintain your 'Playing Coach Man-

agement Style', stay close to your team. Be visible in the organization and avoid being stuck behind your desk and in internal meetings

2. Continue to be yourself and be aware of the enormous risk of becoming overconfident, arrogant and greedy because of your success

3. Keep the strategy 'fresh' and watch out for the unexpected from the competitors you know and the ones that you do not know

4. Avoid "The CEO of the Year Awards." This is the kind of distraction that can lead over confidence and arrogance

5. Focus on your job. Avoid spending more than 10 days per year on external activities including board positions

Go to Chapter 16, where we share our experiences about how to successfully exit from your final CEO job.

HOW TO SUCCESSFULLY EXIT FROM YOUR FINAL CEO JOB

"Getting the job of the CEO is hard. Keeping the job of the CEO is even harder. Retiring from your last job of the CEO is probably the hardest"

Your last big achievement as a successful CEO should be a successful exit from your final CEO job. A disorderly exit is damaging for the company and for you. It will dramatically taint your image/personal brand and decrease your possibilities of having a new successful post-CEO career. You must therefore apply all your skills and experience to master a successful exit.

There is an ideal time to leave your final CEO job!

Leaving your final CEO job, your colleagues and all the excitement, money, joy and prestige that comes with the job is never going to be easy for you. The nature of the job and of successful CEOs means that there will always be another important thing that you want to do. Acquire a major competitor? Launch of a new product? Or God forbid build a new head office? Your successor is not quite ready yet. Your share price is too low. Your options are not in the money. You love the job and everything that comes with it. Leaving a top CEO job is therefore extremely hard.

As mentioned, there will never be an ideal time to leave a top CEO job. It is very complex, because there are so many stakeholders to be taken into account. It is not only about YOU! Your exit is not only important for you and your family, your exit is equally important for the company, for your colleagues, shareholders and other key-stakeholders.

If you decide to make an early and unexpected exit from your CEO job it must be because it is good for the company and for yourself. Good for the company because you have delivered on your promises and because your colleagues will not have time to start playing politics to get your job. Good for you because you can choose to resign, when you are at the top and not when your contract stipulates that you have to retire.

An important pre-condition for a successful *surprise retirement* is that you are financially independent to live the life that you and your family would like after your CEO career. Being an independent chairman, board member or advisor is a pre-condition for maintaining high professional and ethical standards in your future positions.

As the proud and successful CEO that you are, we suggest you consider using the talents that have made you a successful CEO to plan and execute a bold and successful exit from your final CEO job. To help you consider and plan the exit from your dream job we have summarized our experience as a list of 10 subjects that you may want to consider when planning your exit:

1. Be in control of your career. It is better that you take the initiative and plan your exit at a good time than to wait till the chairman tells you that it is time to go or until your contract expires

2. It is not your job to appoint your successor. You should not announce your wish to retire early without offering your thoughts about succession candidates. If you have performed well in your CEO job, there should be one or more internal candidates available as your successor, which means that the transition can be short. If there is no candidate available or the board decides to ask a search firm to look for suitable candidates internally and externally the transition time could be long and painful

3. It is probably not in the best interest of the company that you stay till the very last day of your contract, as this will lead to rivalry and politics between people who think that they should have your job

4. If you want to retire all together from work, you must draw up a plan that supported by your spouse. He or she will probably think that going from a workload of 3,000 hours per year to zero could be bad for both of you. Your spouse will also most probably want assurance that your pension and savings will allow you to maintain your life-style

5. If you want a post-CEO career, we recommend that you have a proper plan in place including a description of your dream positions, a clear personal brand statement and a plan for your work-life balance. If you decide to have a second career, your market value is a function of your exit

6. You can only discuss your plan to resign with your partner and perhaps with a very close friend

7. Never discuss your exit during your tenure. The slightest hint will be damaging for the company and for yourself

8. Do not mention to your chairman that you are considering an early exit. Only tell him or her when you have made

an irreversible decision and when you are ready to hand over your formal resignation letter to him or her. At that time, you are at the point of no return. You can and should discuss the timing, but not your decision. Be generous with timing to avoid putting stress on your chairman and the board. Your resignation letter should motivate why you think that it is good for the company and for you to resign. Your letter should also include a list with the names of your recommended candidates to succeed you

9. To help you making the decision about your early exit we want to remind you that nobody is indispensable!

10. Once your successor is in place, make the transition as short as possible. If he or she is the right choice, you are not needed. If the choice is wrong, it probably does not help to have you around

Our above 10-point list should inspire you to carefully consider, plan and execute your perfectly timed exit. It can pave the way for a new and very exiting second career, where you are more in charge of your life than you have been in your career.

The list is for Group CEOs. We believe that it can also inspire and guide Tier-Two CEOs, who want to master their exit.

CHAPTER 17

DECLINE OR REVIVAL?

When you have climbed the CEO ladder and you fail to get your dream job, you are not a loser. Do not be angry and do not act emotionally. "Stay calm and carry on". Take stock and consider your options by using the common sense and good judgement that has brought you very far in your career.

Now is the time to be CEO of your career and you may want to consider some of the following options:

1. Carry on working loyally in the company under a new boss or perhaps under your old peer and continue to deliver great results. Wait patiently for an unexpected career opportunity that may arise in your company or in another great company

2. Your board may allow you or even encourage you to become non-executive director in one or two companies. This is very interesting for your professional development and could even lead to a CEO job. It is a new trend that non-executives become CEOs in the companies where they serve on the board

3. Switch to an interesting and relevant top specialist executive position in your present company such as head of

M&A, IR, HR or as CEO of the largest region or country away from HQ

4. Become Group CEO of another group in your industry. But not one of your fierce direct competitors. This is not fair to your former company where you have enjoyed a successful career

5. Re-invent yourself, perhaps by making a light double switch, i.e. by becoming Group CEO of a company in a similar industry if your ambition continues being to get a top CEO job

6. If you are at the right age and financially independent, you may consider an early non-executive career as discussed in Chapter 20

The only thing you should not do at this stage is to lose the drive that has shaped your career until this point. If the above has inspired you, we suggest that you revise your career plan and execute it.

CHAPTER 18

WHAT DO YOU DO IF
YOU LOSE YOUR CEO JOB?

INTRODUCTION

If you lose your CEO job you have probably learnt that getting the job of the CEO is very difficult and that keeping it is even more difficult, and that it is a high risk job. Hundreds of CEOs lose their jobs every day. Not always for obvious reasons. CEOs are dismissed, or leave by "mutual consent" to pursue other interests or to spend more time with the family. CEOs of listed companies who lose their jobs attract painful media attention. First time CEOs do generally not attract much attention from the media, when they lose their jobs.

Whether you are a CEO or not, losing your job or being dismissed is dramatic. Telling your family and friends about your dismissal is very painful. It hurts your pride, your social status, you miss your work colleagues, it affects your family and your income, etc. If you lose your CEO job we therefore suggest that you take time to reflect, learn and decide how to move on. The situation varies from person to person, and it plays a role whether you lose your first CEO job, successive CEO jobs or whether you lose a high profile CEO job in a large corporation.

Our experience shows that the vast majority of CEOs who lose their jobs are not very surprised. If you are honest with yourself you should be the first to know, whether your performance is satisfactory or not. Only CEOs that have become arrogant seem to be surprised and angry, when someone dares dismiss them. If your performance has been lagging and if you have had people problems, you will know that this could eventually lead to your dismissal. If this was the case our advise is that you would have been better off, had you resigned from the CEO job before you were dismissed. It will not be easy for you to admit that you are not up to the job. By doing so would spare you the drama of being dismissed.

Depending on the situation, you may have two alternatives for the continuation of your career. The first being that this CEO job is not for you for reasons that you define. You are confident that there are other CEO jobs out there that you will be able to master. The second alternative is that you conclude that the CEO job is not right for you and that you must reorient your career. You may have been over promoted. In either case, you must revisit your career plan and make the necessary changes.

For anyone losing a CEO job there are a number of critical matters that you need to deal with, if you want to minimize the risk of losing jobs in the future. For your inspiration we will go through the ones that we consider important for you to deal with in a manner that corresponds to your own particular situation.

Whatever the reason for your dismissal, we strongly recommend that you behave in such a manner that the company will regard you as a *good leaver*. We mention this, because the way you leave a CEO job will have a major impact on the rest of your career.

FIND OUT WHY YOU LOST YOUR CEO JOB IN AN EXIT INTERVIEW

Once the dust has settled you should ask your company for an exit interview to learn why you were dismissed.

It is critical for the rest of your career that you find the underlying cause of the reasons *why you were dismissed*. The only way you can get full answers to the questions is by asking the people you have worked with. If you openly tell them how important the answers are for the rest of your career, they are likely to help you. You may or may not like the answers. If you are honest with yourself, you will most probably agree with their assessment. For your exit interview, we suggest that you seek to find out, whether your dismissal was due to performance, management style, people or relationship issues, lack of trust or other reasons. In most situations a number of factors, not just one causes a dismissal.

When you get the exit interview, you should try very hard to create a friendly and positive atmosphere as a *good leaver* where you will obtain honest and helpful answers to your questions. We suggest that the below three questions should be included in your list of questions:

Question #1: Why did I lose my job?
During the exit interview and in conversations with colleagues, search consultants, etc. you should try to get as much information as possible about the reasons for your dismissal and the importance of each of them.

Question #2: Which references will you give about me?
You must find out which story they will tell about your exit to your future potential employers. It is unlikely that you will be able to get a new CEO job without an honest reference, which mirrors your own story.

Question #3: Do you recommend that I seek another CEO job?

You probably have your own answer to this question. But it is very important for the future of your career that you get an honest piece of advise from your ex-employer, colleagues and search consultants.

If you cannot get an exit interview with your company, we suggest that you obtain answers to your questions by other means. The most obvious method is to ask some of your close ex-colleagues, the ones that you worked well with and the ones that you did not get along with. Another valuable resource is the search consultants you have known for a longer period. If you want them to help, you move on, they need to get the true version of of your dismissal. Give them your honest version and they will be able to find out, if it were the same, as your company would give to potential new employers. It is very important for your future career that you analyse your mistakes and determine which lessons you must learn to help you minimize the risk of losing future jobs.

REVISE YOUR CAREER PLAN

Based on the results of your exit interview, advise from your search consultants, old colleagues, friends and your spouse it is now time to make a decision about your future career and to prepare a new career plan or to revise the old one. To inspire and guide you, we have in the following listed a number of subjects that you should include in your decision making and planning.

WORK–LIFE BALANCE: Your job and the work-life balance is very important for you and your family. You should therefore talk with your partner about the loss of your job, the short-term consequences, your feelings, the future, etc. and agree about your future work-life balance. In some instances a solution can be that, you take a step back for a while and your partner accelerates his or her career during that period.

SEARCH FIRMS AND NETWORK: Hopefully you have established a partnership with a search consultant as we recommend in Chapter 10. It is in situations like these that you at a very early stage turn to him or her for advise and help, as search firms mostly handle recruitment of senior CEOs. Their perspectives on the loss of your job, their advise and help with a new job could be invaluable for your future career. But remember search consultants are not employment agents. They act on behalf of their clients. In addition, you must activate your network. Tell them what happened and what your new plans are. If they cannot help, they may know people who can. Do it tactfully.

OPTIONS: If the loss of your CEO job indeed was some kind of bad luck which is not likely to happen again, you should be encouraged to look for a new CEO job. You need to know from your ex-boss that he or she agrees that it was indeed bad luck. His or her story must be identical to the story you tell. If both stories are identical and credible, many employers will see the failure in your previous job as one that is likely to stimulate you to do a good job in the future.

If people that you have worked with find that they do not think that you have what it takes to become a successful CEO, you may be disappointed. However, if a group of people who have seen you in action have come to this conclusion, it would be wise to accept their opinion and not go for a new CEO job.

Whatever the reasons behind your dismissal and whatever career you now want to pursue, it is important that you go back to the drawing board to plan and execute a new career plan with the same diligence and energy as in your early career. Given your experience, your successes and failures you should be able to work out a very realistic plan for the rest of your career:

THE CEO CAREER PATH CHART

FUTURE CEOs	PRESENT CEOs	RETIRING CEOs
AGE: 25–35/40	AGE: 35/40–60/65	AGE: 60/65–70/80
WORKING HOURS/YEAR: 3,000	WORKING HOURS/YEAR: 3,000	WORKING HOURS/YEAR: 2,000 → 1,000 → 0
YEARS IN JOBS: 10–15	YEARS IN JOBS: 20–30	YEARS IN JOBS: 10–20
KNOW YOUR CUSTOMERS: ☐ Sales ☐ Marketing ☐ Customer service	CEO JOBS: ☐ S – Small ☐ M – Medium	SECOND CAREER: ☐ Chairman role ☐ Board member ☐ Other roles
KNOW YOUR PRODUCTS: ☐ Operations ☐ Manufacturing ☐ Supply chain ☐ Technology	☐ L – Large ☐ XL – Extra large ☐ XXL – Forbes Global 2000 company	THIRD CAREER: ☐ Board roles ☐ Investor ☐ Mentor ☐ Speaker & writer ☐ Pro-bono roles
KNOW YOUR NUMBERS: ☐ Accounting ☐ Business control ☐ Management consultancy (Strategy and operations)	AN UNEXPECTED EVENT MAKES YOU: ☐ CEO – because you were there as CFO, COO or board member	RETIREMENT: ☐ Pro-bono roles ☐ Investor ☐ Mentor ☐ Other:
☐ Junior management positions		☐ No more business roles

CHAPTER 19

RETIREMENT OR A NEW CAREER?

Like it or not, your CEO career will one day end. You may have had time to get used to the idea, because you have reached your age of retirement, or because you have decided to have an early exit. Or you may have lost your CEO job at an age, where it is unlikely that you can get a new CEO job.

Stepping down from a long and busy career requires careful attention. You must consciously decide whether you want to retire, semi-retire or continue to work.

Our experience shows that only a small minority of CEOs dream of a life with total freedom without the usual workload. If you are one of those, we suggest that you discuss and agree your future life very carefully with your spouse and family. Suddenly having a busy CEO at home is a major change for your spouse, because it affects hers or his life in a very dramatic manner. You should be aware that you might not enjoy your freedom in the way that you had imagined. You run a serious risk of becoming bored with your new-found freedom after 3—6 months, longing to be back in action.

Whatever you decide to do after your CEO career, you must plan and organize your future. You must write a career plan for your second career or a retirement plan.

YOUR POST–CEO OPTIONS ARE:

1. A second full-time career with up to 2,000 working hours per year. This equals 40 weeks p.a. of 40-50 hours per week. Such a career will clearly signal that you have not retired and that you will continue to be a well-informed and attractive chairman or board member. The 1,000 hours that you free up will improve your work life balance

2. A part-time second career with a workload of about 1,000 hours per year will signal that you are semi-retired and you will be considered out of touch with business. A workload of 1.000 hours p.a. equals 40 weeks p.a. 0f 25 hours per week You will free up 2,000 hours per year to hobbies, family, travelling. The number of offers to join boards will decrease considerably and then peter out

3. Full retirement with total freedom. This is an enormous change to your career as CEO. Not one that many CEOs will chose

As mentioned above our experience shows that the vast majority of CEOs dream of doing something meaningful after their CEO careers and therefore chose option 1. If you have been a successful CEO for a long time and have resigned from your CEO job in an orderly manner at the age of around 60, you will be a very attractive chairman and non-executive director.

Your post-CEO market value will peak when you leave your job. If you let the market know that you plan a second career with a portfolio of non-executive jobs, your market value will remain. The market value of a semi-retired CEO is not nearly as high as for a full time ex-CEO. If you let the market know that you want to retire, your market value will diminish to a very low level. You must therefore carefully consider whether you really want to retire or semi-retire.

If you are inclined to go for the full retirement option, we suggest that you write a retirement plan forcing you to think through all aspects and consequences, before you make the final decision together with your spouse.

To help you decide whether a post-CEO career is right for you, we suggest that you establish the motive for the decision. In the self-assessment test no. 1 you assessed the motive for your desire to become a CEO. We think that it will be helpful for you to carry out a similar test regarding your motives for a second career:

MY MOTIVES FOR WANTING A POST-CEO CAREER ARE:			
	ANSWERS	**ANSWERS**	**COMMENTS**
A	I am primarily driven by the urge to make a difference by working with interesting people and projects		
B	I am primarily driven by money and prestige		
C	I need the money		

© 2016 Waldemar Schmidt

If you have answered 'A' you are well suited to start on a post-CEO career with a portfolio of board positions and you should proceed with the planning of your second career.

If you have answered 'B' many chairmen and boards may not regard you as an ideal chairman or board member. You may therefore not be able to get the board positions that you would like.

If you have answered 'C', you will not be independent and therefore not a valuable chairman or board member. You would be best advised to continue in your CEO job till you become financially independent.

We suggest that you revert to your career chart and map out a viable career path to your final executive job or to the end of a second or third career.

THE CEO CAREER PATH CHART

FUTURE CEOs	PRESENT CEOs	RETIRING CEOs
AGE: 25–35/40	AGE: 35/40–60/65	AGE: 60/65–70/80
WORKING HOURS/YEAR: 3,000	WORKING HOURS/YEAR: 3,000	WORKING HOURS/YEAR: 2,000 ➔ 1,000 ➔ 0
YEARS IN JOBS: 10–15	YEARS IN JOBS: 20–30	YEARS IN JOBS: 10–20
KNOW YOUR CUSTOMERS: ☐ Sales ☐ Marketing ☐ Customer service	CEO JOBS: ☐ S – Small ☐ M – Medium	SECOND CAREER: ☐ Chairman role ☐ Board member ☐ Other roles
KNOW YOUR PRODUCTS: ☐ Operations ☐ Manufacturing ☐ Supply chain ☐ Technology	☐ L – Large ☐ XL – Extra large ☐ XXL – Forbes Global 2000 company	THIRD CAREER: ☐ Board roles ☐ Investor ☐ Mentor ☐ Speaker & writer ☐ Pro-bono roles
KNOW YOUR NUMBERS: ☐ Accounting ☐ Business control ☐ Management consultancy (Strategy and operations) ☐ Junior management positions	AN UNEXPECTED EVENT MAKES YOU: ☐ CEO – because you were there as CFO, COO or board member	RETIREMENT: ☐ Pro-bono roles ☐ Investor ☐ Mentor ☐ Other: ☐ No more business roles

CHAPTER 20

HOW TO SUCCEED IN YOUR SECOND CAREER

"Our experience shows that most CEOs are better suited for the chairman role than for the role of an ordinary board member as they are used to taking initiatives, being leaders and making a difference."

© 2016 Waldemar Schmidt

"You would be best advised to continue in your CEO job till you become financially independent before you reconsider a second career."

© 2016 Waldemar Schmidt

"Your post-CEO market value will peak when you leave your job. If you let the market know that you plan a second career with a portfolio of non-executive jobs, your market value will remain. The market value of a semi-retired CEO is not as high as for a CEO with a full-time second career. If you let the market know that you want to retire, your market value will quickly diminish. You must therefore carefully consider whether you really want to semi-retire or retire."

© 2016 Waldemar Schmidt

This chapter is mainly for successful CEOs who have stepped down from their CEO jobs and have appetite for more work in the shape of a second career. It may also inspire other retiring executives who want to pursue a second career.

We know that the vast majority of CEOs who stay in their jobs until the end of their career or till they decide to resign, dream of continuing their active and interesting lives. If you are one of them, you probably have some ideas of what you would like to do.

If you retire from your CEO job at 60 or 65, it is realistic to plan a five to ten year non-executive career. You should however be aware that your market value will be a lot higher at the age of 60 than at the age of 65. If you have enjoyed being a CEO, it is unlikely that you will ever stop doing interesting things. A second career is an opportunity to having a life where you enjoy not having one 24/7 job, but have a portfolio of roles that you can decrease and increase to suit your new work-life balance.

CEOs and chairmen do not keep time sheets. They put in the hours that are required.

TYPICAL WORKLOADS LOOKS LIKE THIS:	
PRE–CEO AND CEO JOBS:	3,000 hours/year 60 – 70 h/week 46 weeks p.a.
SECOND CAREER:	2,000 hours/year 40 – 50 hours/week 40 weeks/year
THIRD CAREER:	1,000-1.600 hours/year 25-40 hours/week 40 weeks/year decreasing to 0 at some point of time

© 2020 Waldemar Schmidt

The workload of a CEO is more or less given. You can now determine how much time you want to spend in your second and third career. There is however a 'risk' that you end up spending more time than you plan in your post-CEO careers. Your companies may be subject to a so called unfriendly takeover, major M&A activities, have management problems, etc. You should therefore leave some time free in your diary.

In the following, we offer some advise for you to consider when preparing for your second career.

HOW TO ORGANIZE YOUR SECOND CAREER

There is a whole range of very important considerations and decisions that you need to make, when you plan your new career and your new life including practical questions like these:

WHERE TO LIVE: You have to consider whether it is time to move to a new place taking your family situation and your future business activities into account. If you want to be very active and have international activities, you should probably live near a major airport.

WORK–LIFE BALANCE: One of the benefits of going from your CEO career to a second career is that you no longer have one all absorbing 24/7 job. You can go from a workload of 3,000 hours per year to 2,000, which gives you a great opportunity to improve your work-life balance. If you decide to have a workload of 2,000 hours per year, people will rightly regard you as fully active. If you decide to go part-time with a workload of say 1,000 hours per year you will be regarded as semi-retired and not quite in touch with business anymore. It is very important that you understand the consequences of these two different post-CEO careers and your market values. For obvious reasons it is very important that you discuss and agree your new work- life balance with your spouse. One of the challenges of a second (and third) career is to distinguish between when you are at work and when you are not. This challenge is further aggravated if your office is at home. Unless you have agreed very clear routines and disciplines with your spouse and family it will be very difficult for them to know, when you are working or not. This is an important theme for you to include in your 'work-life balance plan'.

TITLE: Getting your first CEO business card was very special for you. Losing your final CEO business card is tough, as it has become an important part of your identity. Getting the right new business card for your second career, where you will be building a new identity is therefore important. You will normally use this new card. If you have one or more chairman roles, we suggest that you put the chairman title below your name on your new business card. It is likely that the company where you are the chairman will want to give you one of their business cards with the chairman title to be used when you act for them. If you 'only' have ordinary non-executive positions, you can use the title director below your name. If you decide to set up your own company, you can use the chairman title, the CEO title or both

OFFICE: For most people there are three obvious choices: 1) Set up a fully equipped home office, 2) Share an office with secretarial support with like-minded persons or 3) Use a fully serviced office at a company where you are the chairman.

PA AND IT SUPPORT: This is mainly relevant if you chose to have a home office. However, with modern technology and with part-time secretarial assistance readily available by phone, over the internet or personally, it is easy to get organized. Our experience shows that having IT support can be far more critical than having a PA or PA support.

PERSONAL BRAND: When you start on your second career, we recommend that you update your personal brand statement and include it on your CV clearly stating your competencies as a strong candidate for chairman or non-executive director roles in particular fields. As you will have learnt, it is very important to have a clear and precise personal brand.

DRESS CODE: If you have decided to pursue a second career, you should not show up at board meetings and business meetings dressed as a retired person.

PORTFOLIO: If you have been a successful and respected CEO with a clear personal brand, you will no doubt be contacted about board positions by chairmen, people from your network, search firms and people that you do not know.

You will be invited to give exit interviews by journalists who know you. This is a unique opportunity for you to talk about your plans and wishes for a second career.

We assume that you have decided that an important part of your portfolio should consist of some relevant non-executive positions.

You have experience from working with your chairman and a variety of non-executives on your own board. This will have taught you some useful lessons. You will have worked with board members that you respected and found to be great colleagues. You will probably also have worked with board members that you did not respect and found useless. You should therefore carefully consider how you could use these lessons to help you become a respected and great chairman and non-executive in your second career.

If you already have one or two non-executive positions, you have accumulated valuable non-executive experience for your new career.

In any case, we would like to remind you that the non-executive job is very different from the executive job. You must understand that behaving, as a CEO when you are a non-executive is not going to make you a respected and highly rated board member.

The CEO runs the company. The chairman runs the board. This was true, when you were the CEO and it should be true if/when you become chairman.

DREAM POSITIONS: We suggest that you draw up a list with your dream positions to make it clear to yourself and to search consultants what kind of non-executive roles you would prefer. It is important for you to be clear in your mind, when you start receiving approaches. Be open to approaches from companies, industries and geographies that were not included in your wish list.

CHAIRMAN OR ORDINARY BOARD MEMBER: As already mentioned we know from experience that most CEOs are better suited for the chairman role than for the role as ordinary board member. CEOs are used to taking initiatives. As the chairman of 2-3 companies you can have a much bigger impact than by being an ordinary board member on 4—5 boards.

INDUSTRIES AND COMPANIES: We suggest that you stay away from joining boards of your old competitors although this is where your industry experience lies. If you follow our advise of going for two or three chairman roles you will be in demand as chairman due to your proven 'general management' expertise rather than your industry expertise.

OWNERSHIP: A portfolio can be more interesting when it does not only include publicly listed companies. Sitting on the board of only listed companies can become quite boring. Adding positions in companies with other kinds of ownership such as families, private equity and start-ups will make your work much more interesting and challenging.

GEOGRAPHY: Many boards look for board members with experience from specific countries or continents. When you plan your portfolio, you need to take into account that the workload including travelling to 6—10 annual board meetings in another country or continent increases the time commitment considerably. You may also need to consider language and cultural issues.

COMPANY CHALLENGE: We suggest that you carefully discuss the strategic challenge of the companies that offer you a board seat. For you to be a successful board member there has to be a clear match between your expertise and the expertise that they need in terms of their strategic challenge.

AVOIDING BAD CHOICES: It is crucial that you do everything you can to avoid bad choices. There are many examples of how just one bad choice has ruined a successful ex-CEO's second career and has tainted his or her brand. A thorough and conventional due diligence is necessary. You must find ways to understand the basic of the business, its values, ethical standards and its challenges. Moreover, you must meet all the people that you will work with and make a *judgement* as to whether they are people that you would want to work with. If you are the slightest in doubt, do not do it. You will probably receive many approaches, wherefore you can be critical and say no to more than you say yes to. Experience shows that successful ex-CEOs decline more offers to join boards than they accept.

TIME TO RESIGN: Age or loss of the independent status are not the only reasons to resign from a board. If you disagree with the majority of the board or the owners and you cannot change their minds, you will have to resign. Leaving a board early because you have an opportunity to join the board of a bigger or more prestigious company is bad behaviour.

BOARD FEES: In the same way as you did not choose your CEO career because of the money, you should not chose a non-executive career or a board position because of the money. You do it because you are driven by the urge to make a difference. Our first recommendation is simple, but perhaps ambiguous: You do not take on a role for the money. However, the money has to reflect the time and risk involved. Our second recommendation is that you must be financially independent, so that you can afford to walk away if you disagree with the majority of the board and the owners. From your time as a CEO you have witnessed that the daily rate of a CEO is higher than that of a non-executive. Our advise is therefore that you do not take on board positions for the money, but for the challenge and the opportunity to help the company achieve its goals.

INSURANCE: Do not join a board, which does not offer a comprehensive D&O insurance cover.

APPOINTMENT LETTER: To confirm your appointment, you will normally receive a very formal letter from HR and the legal department about formalities and legalities. If you become chairman, we recommend that you in addition take the initiative to formulate an engagement letter which summarizes all relevant details and understandings about the company's strategy, the expectations to you and any other issue that you find of importance.

OTHER ROLES: Sitting on boards is not the only option that you have in your second career. Depending on your interests, you may enjoy teaching at business schools, writing books, giving speeches, investing in and sitting on boards of start-ups, working with private equity firms, NGOs, etc.

THIRD CAREER: A decision about a possible third career has to be made as carefully as the one you made for your second career. If your second career runs over a ten-year period there will inevitably be a certain turnover of your roles. Companies can merge, be taken over or you may resign. If you wish to have a third career you may want to decrease your workload and find roles that are well suited for you as we discuss in Chapter 21.

THE CEO CAREER PATH CHART

FUTURE CEOs	PRESENT CEOs	RETIRING CEOs
AGE: 25–35/40	AGE: 35/40–60/65	AGE: 60/65–70/80
WORKING HOURS/YEAR: 3,000	WORKING HOURS/YEAR: 3,000	WORKING HOURS/YEAR: 2,000 ➜ 1,000 ➜ 0
YEARS IN JOBS: 10–15	YEARS IN JOBS: 20–30	YEARS IN JOBS: 10–20
KNOW YOUR CUSTOMERS: ☐ Sales ☐ Marketing ☐ Customer service	CEO JOBS: ☐ S – Small ☐ M – Medium	SECOND CAREER: ☐ Chairman role ☐ Board member ☐ Other roles
KNOW YOUR PRODUCTS: ☐ Operations ☐ Manufacturing ☐ Supply chain ☐ Technology	☐ L – Large ☐ XL – Extra large ☐ XXL – Forbes Global 2000 company	THIRD CAREER: ☐ Board roles ☐ Investor ☐ Mentor ☐ Speaker & writer ☐ Pro-bono roles
KNOW YOUR NUMBERS: ☐ Accounting ☐ Business control ☐ Management consultancy (Strategy and operations) ☐ Junior management positions	AN UNEXPECTED EVENT MAKES YOU: ☐ CEO – because you were there as CFO, COO or board member	RETIREMENT: ☐ Pro-bono roles ☐ Investor ☐ Mentor ☐ Other ☐ No more business roles

CHAPTER 21

HOW TO SUCCEED IN YOUR THIRD CAREER

Although we live longer and longer, companies in many countries have Corporate Governance Recommendations that stipulate your 70 years' birthday as the age where you can no longer serve as an independent non-executive director of a publicly listed company. The vast majority of companies 'comply' with these recommendations. Very few have the courage to 'explain' when a director who is fit to continue in spite of his age.

If you are fit and want to continue working with interesting things, you should not despair when you start losing your non-executive positions in publicly listed companies around your 70th birthday. There are many things you can do, to if you want an exciting third career. But as in your early career and when you stepped down from your CEO job we recommend that you reflect over your wishes and possibilities before you write the career plan for your third career.

It is likely that you want to slow down a bit to improve the work-life balance. It is our experience that many ex-CEOs are still not ready to give up working, when they turn 70.

Reducing your workload in your third career would probably classify you as semi-retired. At this stage in your life it will not affect the types of roles that you will be offered.

The practicalities around your third career such as location of your office, business cards, office support, etc. remain more or less the same as they were in your second career.

The structure of your career plan for your third career can very much follow the format that we recommended for your second career plan in Chapter 20.

To facilitate the planning of your third career we have summarized our experience in the below additional subjects for you to consider:

HOW MUCH TIME DO YOU WANT TO COMMIT: Most ex-CEOs will want a further reduction of their work load in their third career. You may start with 1,500 hours per year and gradually scale down. 1.500 hours be year equals a full time job in certain countries. For a non-executive it could equal 30-40 hours per week 40 weeks p.a. This will feel as quite 'light' for most ex-CEOs although it almost corresponds to a standard full-time job.

FEES: In most instances, board fees and workloads are lower than you have been used to.

COMPLEXITY OF PORTFOLIO: We think of complexity in terms of the number of roles that you take on, the responsibility of each role, the travelling required, the number of industries you have to understand, the issues in private companies versus issues in public companies, etc. As you grow older, we suggest that you should reduce the complexity of your work from the start of your third career and during your third career. Your work at this time of your life should be challenging, but also fun. It should not be stressful and burdensome. You can still be involved in interesting things and make a difference.

NON-EXECUTIVE ROLES: You will probably feel relieved to escape from the big formal board room with its strict annual routines and corporate governance rules, up to 10 annual board meetings, budgets, monthly, quarterly, half-year and full year review, annual reports, audit committee, remuneration committee, AGM, etc. Leaving the public company world is a great opportunity to have more fun in your third career.

If you have prepared yourself well for the third career, you should already have some 'fun' roles. As to additional new roles, we suggest that you are open-minded and consider our advise. Draw up a list with your dream roles and positions to make it clear to yourself what kind of roles you prefer and which one you do not want. You should not expect to get as much help from your search firms as you did when you started on your second career. Your network and your own initiative must be activated.

Our experience is that one chairman role in a relevant privately owned company, where you can make a real difference, should be your anchor position. Such a position is equally important for the owners of the company, for your status and for your business card.

You could add some additional ordinary board positions to your portfolio if the requirements correspond to your specific skills and you therefore can take on the responsibility for one or more special projects.

INVESTING: Many ex-CEOs find it fascinating to invest in and help start-up companies. Many entrepreneurs find it extremely useful to be mentored by a seasoned and successful ex-CEO. Working with young entrepreneurs at this stage of your career can therefore be mutually beneficial. The entrepreneurs have the ideas and the energy. You have the experience and maybe some cash to invest. You should also find time to look after you own finances.

PRO-BONO: There are many pro-bono organizations who can benefit greatly from ex-CEOs' leadership and organizational skills. For ex-CEOs taking on a board role or just giving some advise is very often a very positive experience for both parties.

ADVICING: It is our experience that ex-CEOs find it very hard 'only' to be advisors. It is in their DNA to take initiatives and to make decisions. A role on an advisory board can however sometimes be a great opportunity for ex-CEOs to improve their skills in the art of influencing.

CONSULTING: It is also our experience that most ex-CEOs don't enjoy consulting roles for two reasons. The first one being that they are not used to selling their services as time measured in hours or days. The daily rate of ex-CEOs often exceed the fees of top consultants. The second reason is that CEOs have become CEOs because their 'metier' is to lead and to make decisions.

SPEAKING: Some ex-CEOs are engaged by speaking bureaus to give speeches at seminars and conferences and/or asked by business schools to give lectures. This can be very stimulating and a great component of your portfolio in your second and third career. Our experience is that an ex-CEO should not make speeches about his or her old company, unless the company explicitly asks them to do so. They should stick to talking about subjects that are contained in their personal brand.

COACHING: It is common place that successful ex-CEOs are approached by people they know and by people they don't know for career and business advise. It is our experience that in particular people who lost their CEO jobs or who want to build a non-executive career enjoy and benefit from talking with ex-CEOs. We recommend that you should be open to such approaches and always answer the caller. You may not always have time for a meeting. You will have time for a call. Being approachable should continue to be part of your personal brand.

GEOGRAPHY: Having worked globally it is not likely that you will enjoy working only locally. On the other hand having had your fair share of jetting around the globe, you will probably want to limit the number of 'foreign' roles that you take on in your third career.

A third career, which as mentioned starts with a workload of 1,500 hours per year, which will allow you to have the best work-life balance you have had since your school days. Do not miss the opportunity to make a wonderful 'work-life plan' with your spouse and family.

Finally, for many reasons it is very difficult to determine the length of your third career. Even for successful ex-CEOs, it will be wise to scale down gradually as you complete some of your 'missions'. And for your personal pride, don't stay too long in any position. With your background and experience, you should continue to judge and decide when it is time to go. You do not want to be dismissed from any roles at this point of time of your career!

For the planning of your 3rd career you may be inspired by looking at our chart for the last time:

THE CEO CAREER PATH CHART

FUTURE CEOs	PRESENT CEOs	RETIRING CEOs
AGE: 25–35/40	AGE: 35/40–60/65	AGE: 60/65–70/80
WORKING HOURS/YEAR: 3,000	WORKING HOURS/YEAR: 3,000	WORKING HOURS/YEAR: 2,000 ➔ 1,000 ➔ 0
YEARS IN JOBS: 10–15	YEARS IN JOBS: 20–30	YEARS IN JOBS: 10–20
KNOW YOUR CUSTOMERS: ☐ Sales ☐ Marketing ☐ Customer service	CEO JOBS: ☐ S – Small ☐ M – Medium	SECOND CAREER: ☐ Chairman role ☐ Board member ☐ Other roles
KNOW YOUR PRODUCTS: ☐ Operations ☐ Manufacturing ☐ Supply chain ☐ Technology	☐ L – Large ☐ XL – Extra large ☐ XXL – Forbes Global 2000 company	THIRD CAREER: ☐ Board roles ☐ Investor ☐ Mentor ☐ Speaker & writer ☐ Pro-bono roles
KNOW YOUR NUMBERS: ☐ Accounting ☐ Business control ☐ Management consultancy (Strategy and operations) ☐ Junior management positions	AN UNEXPECTED EVENT MAKES YOU: ☐ CEO – because you were there as CFO, COO or board member	RETIREMENT: ☐ Pro-bono roles ☐ Investor ☐ Mentor ☐ Other: ☐ No more business roles

© 2020 Waldemar Schmidt

CHAPTER 22

HOW TO SUCCEED WITH YOUR WORK–LIFE BALANCE

The big work-life question at all times during your career is whether you can have a long and successful CEO career with 3,000 hours per year and at the same time have a happy family life?

"The answer is YES! But only if you and your spouse plan your work-life balance in the same diligent manner as you plan your career and only if you master your CEO job. We argue that it is very difficult or perhaps even impossible to have a long and successful CEO career without also having a happy family life."

We illustrate our work-life balance experience and belief with our *virtuous work-life balance circle*:

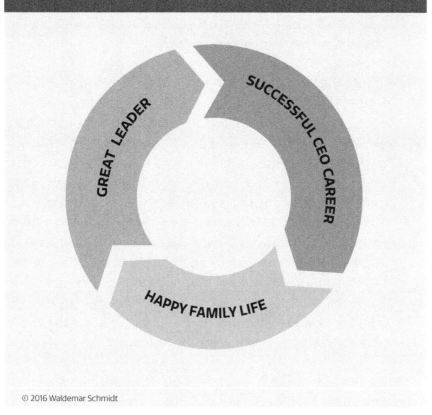

THE VIRTUOUS WORK–LIFE BALANCE CIRCLE

SUCCESSFUL CEO CAREER

GREAT LEADER

HAPPY FAMILY LIFE

© 2016 Waldemar Schmidt

The alternative is *the vicious work-life balance circle*, which can be originated by any of its three components. Needless to say that you must avoid the vicious circle.

Our experience has taught us that the subject of work-life balance is very individual and very difficult to summarize in a number of tips. We do not think that there is a magic formula, which will enable you to eliminate the challenges of your work-life balance. There are many books available about the subject. You can find many lists with *"Tips for work-life balance"* on the internet.

We have three recommendations for you to consider:

1. Take on jobs that stretch you to your limit. Do not take on jobs that stress you beyond your limit

2. In addition to your career plans, we recommend that you develop short, but carefully worded work-life balance plans at each stage of your career. A work-life balance plan is not a spreadsheet exercise. It requires much more EQ than IQ. Your *goals, priorities, sacrifices* and *trade-offs* are a consequence of your career choices. Defining and agreeing the trade-off is normally the most difficult part. It is paramount that you both understand and accept that there is a price to be paid, if you want to have a successful CEO career with 3,000 working hours per year. You cannot have one or two ambitious careers between you and your spouse and at the same time have lots of time for hobbies and friends. Couples with two careers normally have the financial means to pay domestic help to get the work-life balance, they desire

3. We recommend that you follow-up, review and adjust your private work-life balance plan on a regular yearly basis. Very importantly at every career move, you and your spouse must discuss and agree to the consequences that the move will have on your work-life balance. It is at least as important to follow-up on your work-life balance plan as it is to follow up on your career plans and on the business plans in your company

CHAPTER 23

HOW TO DEAL WITH CRITICAL CAREER AND JOB DILEMMAS

THE A – Z CEO CAREER GUIDE

This objective of this chapter is to be your source of inspiration about key leadership and career issues that both young and mature leaders will face during their entire working lives. There are, however no black-and-white solutions to complex issues. Our purpose is to inspire and to help you find your own way in dealing with a number of common critical issues. We recommend that you carefully read and reflect over each issue when reading the entire book for the first time. This will put you in the right mood to plan and execute your CEO career.

ACCIDENTPRONE: Certain people seem to be accident-prone. Their CVs typically reveal a sequence of short stints at many companies without any logical progression—no red thread. When asked why they left their jobs, they usually answer that the company was restructured or that their boss left or the company was acquired. This leaves questions as to why a particular individual was the loser. Did he or she do a bad job or make a bad judgement call when he or she joined that company? Regardless, the lesson is clear: Don't hire people who seem to be accident-prone.

ACCOUNTANTS: You often meet the argument that accountants will never become great leaders. Wrong! If accountants have the characteristics of great, leaders and they decide to manage as general managers and not as accountants, they can well become great leaders.

ACCOUNTABILITY: The more people you can make truly accountable for their business units or functions, the higher your odds of delivering your budgets will be. And delivering your budgets is a key to being promoted.

ACQUISITIONS: Making acquisitions is probably the easiest of all business disciplines. You just pay the price that the seller wants! Moreover, acquisitions are regarded by many executives as one of the most exciting elements of their role. Making acquisitions is also the most difficult of all business disciplines. Just look at the statistics showing that many acquisitions fail to deliver value. Acquisitions often go wrong in one or more of the following areas: 1) The acquirer does not have acquisition experience and a proper acquisition strategy; 2) There is no robust 'take-over and integration plan' in place; 3) An overambitious CEO simply acquires the wrong company.

ADVISORS: You should never believe that you are a specialist in everything. Therefore the use of advisors and consultants can be crucial in certain very special situations. Ultimately, however, never forget that advisors are advisors: they provide you with good advise. You are an executive and you make decisions and execute with your colleagues.

AGGRESSIVE: A Chinese MBA student at IMD once came to me with a question. His classmates said that he was not aggressive enough to become a CEO. What did I think? Based on my experience, I told him that I do not think that successful leaders are aggressive; rather, they are energetic, persuasive and team players, etc.

AMBITIONS: You must have ambitions if you want to be successful in business, but you should not only have *personal* ambitions. To move up the career ladder, your ambitions must include ambitions for your team, for your business unit and, very importantly, for your company. When discussing your ambitions with your boss, you should not only ask the question, 'What can the company do for me?' but also 'What can I do for the company?'

ANALYSTS: Many executives disrespectfully refer to financial analysts as '25 year old number crunchers with no clue about their business'. You should never talk disrespectfully about anybody—and definitely not about one of your key stakeholders. We take a different view of analysts. A financial analyst is a stakeholder in the company. We listen to all stakeholders when we formulate company strategy or make very large business decisions. We therefore also listen to financial analysts.

ANALYSES: We know an ex-CFO who spent most of his career working for one of the world's 500 largest companies. He told us something very interesting about the two CEOs he had worked with. The first one made sure that he had all-critical facts right. He then used his team and his judgement to make decisions. The second one was a maniac with numbers. He always wanted yet another analysis before he made big decisions—and only reluctantly at that. He kept searching for the truth in the figures. Lessons learnt: You must intimately understand and know your business and what drives it; you must know and understand the numbers; you will never find the truth in numbers.

ANSWERS: When asked a question, answer it to the point. Do not start telling everything you know about the subject.

ARROGANCE: Probably the worst enemy of great leadership. If arrogance is an ingrained component of your DNA and you cannot get rid of it, it is highly unlikely that you will have a long career in leading positions. Arrogance does not only stem from your DNA. Successful leaders often become arrogant because of their success. They do not notice. If arrogance is part of your DNA, you must understand and accept that people see you as arrogant. Thereafter, you must make an effort to change your behaviour and arrange that someone you trust and respect polices your behaviour and gives you honest feedback on your progress in order to ensure you lose the arrogant style. In many cases, your spouse or partner would be the best person to help you with this very delicate task. In order to avoid arrogance creeping in because of your success, you are well advised to avoid becoming a 'Celebrity CEO' who spends excessive time outside the company on boards, giving speeches at conferences, appearing in the media and ending up as 'Manager of the Year'. Your spouse or partner should help you to remain the genuine person you were, when you got the CEO job.

ATTITUDE: Great leaders have a positive attitude.

AVAILABILITY: Great leaders are always available when needed. Some people lock themselves in their office for a week with a 'Do not disturb' sign on the door when they work on a particular project. Some of these people have the ambition to get a leadership position; however, they usually don't make it. However, they are often terrifically valuable specialists as a one-man team. Being available does not mean that you answer mails and calls on your Blackberry or iPhone, when you are in meetings or with people. When you are with people, you are 100% available to them. However, you should organize your day in such a way that there are enough slots to deal with urgent mails and urgent calls. We know many CEOs who have their email address, mobile number and private phone number printed on their business card, and they tell us that this trust is never abused because they have trained people around them to understand how they work.

BALANCED SCORECARD: This is one of the very few buzz words that you will find in this book. Balanced score cards can be extremely effective, if they are kept simple and transparent. Five KPIs—of which three are financial and two are non-financial—are sufficient in focusing on the running of even the largest and most complex businesses. Furthermore, balanced score cards can form the basis for incentive systems.

BEHAVIOUR: Some top leaders start to believe that they are so brilliant and powerful that they are above the law. You have become a CEO because of who you are. Keep learning and keep developing your skills. Never assume that laws do not apply to you.

BIGGER JOB IN SMALLER COMPANIES: You should be aware that getting a bigger job in a smaller company can be difficult. In a very large company, executives are supported by and dependent upon lots of staff functions. This means that you get specialist advise on all major decisions. You sometimes also have matrix situations where you are not truly independent in your decision-making. A move from a job as regional CEO in a large company to a position as CEO in a smaller company can therefore be very difficult. If such a move is a double switch, where you move up one level and change industry, you should be aware that the risk of failure for you and your new employer is considerable. The job, as CEO of a small or medium-sized company, is much more hands-on than a job as regional CEO in a large company. Many employers and owners of small and medium sized companies dream of employing a top executive from a large global firm without being aware of the risk of failure.

BLACK OR WHITE: Great leaders do not see business issues as either black or white. It is not as simple as that. Some managers do apply the B/W management concept, but generally without success. If things were that straightforward, leaders would be unnecessary—accountants and computers could be in charge.

Another variant that we do not recommend is a concept that was applied by a chemical engineer who became a CEO. He believed that, by breaking business issues down to the smallest particles, he could find the right answers to his problems.

BLAME GAME: Playing the blame game is a no-no if you want to become a great leader. If something goes wrong for you, you do not blame somebody else. You are accountable and you have to face the problem. Good bosses can take bad news — as long as it is explained properly. Therefore, go to your boss as early as possible to explain what went wrong, why it went wrong, what you have learnt and, very importantly, how and when you are going to fix it. Great leaders take the blame when something goes wrong and attribute successes to their teams.

BOARDS: In your early career, you will probably not have much exposure to the board and what it does. However, as you take on more senior positions, this will change. You may be involved in preparing papers for the board, and you may even be asked to make a presentation to the board. You should know that this happens mainly when the board wants exposure to talents, so you should be extremely well prepared if you are invited to present something to the board. Joining the board is something very special: it is recognition, it feels great, and you become involved in key decisions surrounding strategy, people issues, etc. One way of learning about the work in boards is to join the board of another company as a non-executive. Invitations for this usually come from search firms, which is one more reason, why you should find one or two search firms to work with throughout your career. They prefer to propose candidates that they know well. Being a non-executive of a board will make you a better executive in terms of working with your own board.

BONUS: Must be simple and transparent to ensure that it serves its purpose, i.e. incentivize managers and staff to achieve extraordinary results. Many bonus programs are far too complicated, short-term and difficult to monitor during the year.

BOTTLENECK: One of the clear signs of a micromanager is when he or she becomes a bottleneck. You must avoid this. Get your priorities right and deal with matters with appropriate urgency. Trust your people and let them get on with their work.

BUDGETS: Budgets must be stretched, but achievable. Delivering or exceeding your budgets year after year is career enhancing.

BUILDING TEAMS: Great leaders understand the importance of having great teams with complementary skills around them. They know how to recruit, develop and retain their team members. They are not afraid of giving people challenging jobs.

BULLDOZING: Bulldozing may do the job. However, it causes a lot of damage, wherefore it is not a technique that is applied by great leaders.

BULLYING: The use of primitive means, such as bullying, will not make you a long-lasting successful CEO. Only weak people who fear losing their jobs put up with bullies. You want smart and independent people around you; therefore, you must stay away from bullying wherever in the world your work takes you! Moreover, if your subordinates are incurable bullies, consider weeding them out: remember that it only takes one bad apple to sour the barrel.

CASH: Companies go broke when they run out of cash. You can only pay your bills with cash. Not with EBITDA. Make sure that your business makes real money, i.e. cash.

CELEBRATE: Celebrate your successes and you will have more of them.

CELEBRITY CEO: When CEOs lose focus on running their business it could be because they have fallen into the celebrity CEO trap. The business world is littered with so-called 'Celebrity CEOs'. They are *perceived* to be successful by the media, but often not so by their shareholders and colleagues. Nobody dares 'touch' them. The symptoms are that their results and achievements are declining. However, they speak well, address all sorts of conferences, sit on too many boards, spend too much time with politicians, are media darlings, and have an opinion about everything. They have their biographies written, become 'Manager of the Year', go to all sorts of receptions, cocktail parties, etc. All of this activity means the company's performance suffers. Somebody must stop them as soon as the symptoms start to appear. This is the job of the chairman, the spouse/partner or a close friend. When CEOs become 'celebrity CESs' they lose focus. It is therefore a good time for shareholders to consider selling their shares.

CEO: The CEO title is relatively new. Initially, it was only used for Group CEOs but is now used widely. The easy way of getting the title is to start your own company—although building your own company is not at all easy. There are companies with 100 country CEOs, 5—10 regional CEOs and one Group CEO. The move from tier four to tier three where you get your first CEO title requires a lot of hard work and outstanding performance. The move from tier three CEO to tier two CEO is much, much harder, but one that you can try to plan for. The top job, Group CEO of a large company is not one that you can plan for. There are far too many unknown factors.

CHARISMA: A certain amount of charisma is good and necessary, if you want to become a successful CEO. However, if your charisma is huge, and is your main characteristic, it will probably hinder you in pursuing a life as a long-lasting successful CEO. You must also be able to deliver.

COACHING: Be wary of a senior person who wants and needs personal coaching. The vast majority of great leaders have not reached their position by being coached. Use coaching with care and generally only for junior executives for very specific purposes and during a limited period.

COLLEAGUES: Only the group CEO and the chairman can pick all of their team members. This means everybody else will have to work with many people that they themselves have not selected. This means that you will have to work with colleagues that range from friends to people who never will be your friends. As long as you are colleagues, are competent and do a great job, you must put your personal opinion aside and work well with everybody.

COMMAND: Some leaders believe that you must give orders to people. "You do not command people to do a good job. You inspire people to do a good job." It is a great philosophy whether you deal with a security guard or one of your nearest colleagues.

COMMUTING: As a global executive, there may well be periods where you have to commute between your home in one country and your office in another; however, you should not do this for very long. Staff in, office may see you as a stranger or not part of the team if you fly away every Friday afternoon and return on Monday mornings. Furthermore, it is very likely that your family will also see you as a stranger or weekend guest.

COMPETITORS: Many business people tend to underestimate their competitors. If you have been involved in acquiring competitors, you may have been positively surprised by the strengths of the acquired competitor. Therefore, never underestimate the competition.

COMPLICATING: Many managers have a tendency to complicate matters. One of the characteristics of great leaders is their ability to keep things simple. Spend time and effort on untangling complicated matters before you present them to your team or colleagues. Moreover, teach them to do likewise.

CONFIDENCE: You must have a lot of confidence in your colleagues. However, you should never be overconfident in yourself.

CONFLICTS: Real problems do not go away by themselves, and they take focus away from running the business. You must deal with them in a positive manner and not be shy of a potential conflict, however unpleasant at the time.

CONSULTANTS: There are times when it is very wise to use consultants. Nevertheless, it is essential that you always remember that you retain consultants to give you advise. You listen to their advise and you run the business.

CONTINOUS IMPROVEMENT: Mark Twain's quote "Continuous improvement is better than delayed perfection" is also very relevant in the business world.

CONTROL FREAK: Control freaks and micromanagers will never be long-term successful CEOs. You must of course, have control mechanisms in your business via internal and external audit and business controllers—but not armies of them. The bulk of control should be incorporated within the business model with total transparency through as many as possible profit centres. Having many profit centres can create many CEO jobs, and it makes your great managers and their teams accountable, since it shows you who performs and delivers results.

COPYCATS: Leaders do not copy what other people do, but they are often inspired by what other people do. Do not try to copy the way Jack Welsh ran GE in the last millennium; rather be inspired and do things your own way.

CORPORATE GOVERNANCE: Corporate governance became the flavour of the month after the Enron scandal in 2001. It is unavoidable. For many board members, this became the first tangible tool that they could work with. It should be ensured that the board work is balanced appropriately between business issues and corporate governance.

CORPORATE WORKER: A corporate worker could be an executive who has spent a long time in a large corporation surrounded, and supported by loads of specialist staff who need to be consulted about every major business decision. Moving away from such an environment to a smaller firm or, 'worse still', becoming an entrepreneur, often proves almost impossible. Therefore, if you start a career as a corporate worker, you must make an early decision as to the duration of your tenure in that company. If you stay for a very long time, then you should probably stay put or possibly move to an equally sized company in the same industry. Starting out your career with three to six years as a corporate worker will teach you the value of excellence. Achieving great results during your tenure will also benefit your future career.

CORRECTIVE ACTIONS: If 'something' (results, projects, etc.) do not go to plan, you must always come up with corrective action (Plan B) when you report the bad news to your boss. Bosses like solutions, not problems. A good boss will, in most instances accept your Plan B, as long as it is credible and as long as it does not happen too often.

CORRUPTION: Great leaders stay away from dealings which require unethical behaviour. Corruption is not only cancer of society. It is cancer of business.

COUNTRY CEO: Being country CEO in a global company is often a wonderful job with lots of freedom as long as you perform. A great start of a CEO career can often be to become country CEO at a young age in a small but fast growing business far away from the head office. You will be able to build a young team of great local people and you will be so close to the business and all its functions that you will acquire the skills that you need in finance, sales & marketing, human resources, supply chain, etc. Doing a great job in such, a situation will naturally be noticed by your bosses. Small businesses in new markets often attract a lot of attention from HQ. This, in turn, results in a disproportionate amount of visits from HQ, which is a great way of building your brand. The next career moves will often be a series of bigger and bigger country CEO jobs. Subsequently, the inevitable often happens: you become EVP at HQ, which can be very difficult, because you become a number two man and lose your freedom.

CRITICISM: You must never criticize a subordinate in public. If he or she is not up to the job and you have tried to help him or her to improve, there is only one solution: he or she must move on.

CRS: Corporate social responsibility is about decent behaviour, displayed by the corporation and its people. It is not a department at head office (though these exist). It must be embedded in your corporation's way of doing business.

CULTURES: In a global company, you have different cultures spanning from religion to food, dress code, language, personal behaviour, etc. It goes without saying that cultural differences must be respected. Teams comprising different cultures enhance performance. Our experience is that the best way to unify a workforce of many different cultures is to have strong and meaningful values and a clear vision, which tells every employee why his or her work is so important for the company to achieve its goals. However, fine words have to be put into practice and the issue of culture must never stand in the way of careers.

CUSTOMERS: Whatever your job, you should always serve customers well, listen to them, and stay close to them.

DEAL-MAKING: Making deals is not a core management discipline. Deal making seems to be a well-developed commercial instinct, which certain people are born with. Brilliant dealmakers are rarely great leaders who become successful CEOs over long periods. Dealmakers and serial entrepreneurs seem to share some of the same qualities.

DECISION-MAKING: As a leader, your job is to make decisions. You often need to decide between two or more proposals that look equally good. You must have the ability to make sound judgements once you have all relevant facts available and you have listened to your team. You will experience that implementation of 'our decision' is usually more successful than 'my decision'.

DELIVER: If you are reliable and deliver on your promises, you will have great career prospects. Ensure that your deadlines, budgets, targets and objectives are all ambitious, but realistic to make sure you have a chance to deliver.

DIVERSITY: We all have a strange tendency to recruit people similar to ourselves. However, we must remind ourselves that diverse teams produce much better results than teams where all members have the same profile as ourselves.

DOUBLE SWITCH: A 'double switch career move' is when you switch industry and move up one step on the organizational career ladder, i.e. from Country CEO in the pharmaceutical industry to Group CEO in the IT industry. Both you and your new employer must be conscious of the considerable risk that such a move incurs.

DRIVE: You must have drive (meaning a blend of determination and ambition to achieve set goals) to be a great leader, and you must surround yourself with people who are also driven.

EGO: Make sure that you do not have a big ego, as big egos do not become great leaders with long-term success as CEOs.

ENERGY: If you want to be a successful CEO you must have a lot of positive energy and the ability to energize your team. Lazy people do not become great leaders.

ENGAGEMENT LETTER: Chairmen do not usually have employment contracts. They have very formal appointment letters in strict legal language. We suggest that chairmen in addition and after thorough due diligence should write an engagement letter in which they summarize all relevant details about the job that they are hired to perform, including the expectations to them.

ENGAGEMENT MEMO: CEOs have formal employment contracts. In addition, we recommend that CEOs write an engagement letter to their boss in which they summarize all relevant details about the job that they are hired to perform including what is expected from them.

ENGINEERS: You often meet the argument that engineers will never become great leaders. Wrong! If engineers have the characteristics of great leaders and they decide to manage as General Managers and not as engineers, they can well become great leaders.

ENTREPRENEURS: With the emergence of the internet a new breed of entrepreneurs has appeared. The serial entrepreneur ('the build to exit'). Many serial entrepreneurs seem to be driven by the urge to develop a business to a certain stage, to make money and then move on to the next project. The old-fashioned entrepreneur ('the build to last entrepreneur') is driven by the urge to create and develop a sustainable business. If you set out to become an entrepreneur, it is important that you decide whether you want to become a 'build to exit' entrepreneur or a 'build to last' entrepreneur because the management concepts to be applied are very different.

ENTREPRENEURSHIP: Successful CEOs of large global corporations are often corporate workers with a certain amount of entrepreneurship DNA, combined with the attributes of great leaders.

EVALUATION: Everybody likes to know how he or she is doing and whether or not his or her boss is happy with their performance. This is particularly the case for ambitious leaders. The best way to measure performance is to have a transparent performance-based business system, where performance is measured continuously in the monthly profit & loss, on a project-by-project basis, etc. Having a performance-based business system has many advantages, one of which is to ensure that all managers always know whether they are doing a good job or a bad job. This will avoid big surprises when formal evaluations are made.

EXCUSES: There are no excuses in business. You give explanations followed by what you have learnt, what you have done or what you will do about it.

EXECUTIVE SEARCH FIRMS: A vulgar term for executive search firms is head-hunters. The five leading global executive search firms do much more than executive search; they also do board consulting, leadership strategy services, CEO succession, family business advisory and diversity and inclusion advisory work. In the early stage of your career, you will mostly be interested in the executive search services. However, as you progress, you will become interested in their other services. As with all consultants, the better they know you and the better you know them, the more they can advise and assist you. Therefore, early on in your career you should select a firm to be sparring and working with throughout your entire working life.

EXPATRIATES: There was a time where large multinational corporations had expatriate managers from their home country in all key jobs around the world. We believe this had to do with lack of trust in locals and a shortage of local talents. More and more global companies have learnt that this concept is outdated, demotivating for local talent, and expensive. Some still use expatriates but for different reasons, such as in the form of a training ground for high-potentials and the transfer of values and know-how.

EXPECTATIONS: Successful CEOs are great at managing expectations of all their stakeholders. They make sure that expectations are well defined and met or exceeded.

EXTERNAL OFFERS: During their careers all great executives receive approaches from search consultants or directly from other firms with job opportunities.

EXTERNAL RECRUITMENT: When an external candidate is chosen over an internal candidate, you must always make sure that he or she is seen as much more suitable by the internal candidates who did not get the job. External recruitment is often made when change is on the agenda.

FAILURE AS CEO: CEOs usually fail for one or more of the following reasons: micromanagement, lack of courage and decisiveness to make critical decisions, arrogance, big ego, aggression or inability to withstand pressure. Each of these characteristics makes it impossible to build a strong team and therefore to produce great results.

FAMILY OWNED COMPANIES: In many family-owned or family-controlled companies, it can be a big challenge to make appointments to the top positions. The tendency is often to prefer family members in all key roles—at least for the first few generations. If you consider joining a family-owned company, you should discuss your career potential, i.e. whether there is a glass ceiling somewhere in the hierarchy. If you are the chairman or CEO of a family-owned company wanting to recruit an external CEO, you should be aware how difficult such a transition is for 'corporate workers'.

FAST TRACK: In the on-going 'battle for talent', more and more large global companies have some kind of fast-track programme for high-potentials. At the same time, more and more young men and women with CEO ambitions make their own career plans and develop personal brands. When planning to hop onto the career ladder, there is the need to explore how you can get in contact with companies whose 'fast-track programs for high potentials' match your own career plan and the personal brand you want to develop.

FAULT: In business—and for that matter in all relations between people—it is not about 'whose fault it is'. It is about taking responsibility. Fault assigning and finger pointing are not good terms in business.

FEAR: No organization performs well in an atmosphere of fear. Fear appears in two different ways. One is where bosses instil a climate of fear. This is obviously not conducive to the working climate and consequently to performance. The other is where leaders are fearful of making decisions—tough or otherwise. Leaders who instil fear in their organizations and leaders who are fearful of making decisions will not become great leaders.

FINISHED: Some people unconsciously work with three versions of the word 'finished' when asked if they have finished the project for which you are waiting eagerly. You have 'almost finished', 'finished' and 'completely finished'. Being able to tell your boss that your project is 'completely finished' will benefit your career.

FIRE: Don't use the term 'you're fired' except if someone has been dishonest and you want the whole organization to know that dishonesty is not tolerated. You can use so many other terms, if you have to tell a member of your team that he or she will have to move on. Surprisingly, you will often find that underperformers know that they are not in the right place and are often relieved, when the pain is over.

FOCUS: Successful CEOs have a very strong and continuous focus on their jobs, but not to the extent that it becomes paranoia.

FRIENDS: Employing friends is nepotism. Becoming friends with colleagues is positive for the climate in the office and should not prevent professional behaviour.

FUN: You should always strive to create a workplace that has an element of fun; this helps performance. A good atmosphere is conducive to good results—your team will benefit if people enjoy going to work.

FUNCTIONAL EXPERTISE: Most executives start their careers with one functional expertise. This could be finance, marketing, engineering or some other competence. If you want to move into general management with the ambition to become a successful CEO, gaining functional expertise in functions that you did not study at university is essential. A successful CEO has expertise in finance, marketing and supply chain, manufacturing and operations. This enables you to understand all business issues and your colleagues will not waste your time by arguing that 'this does not work with the customer in production or in finance.' You simply become a complete CEO by having functional expertise in all key areas of your business. This argument also supports our view that you should not switch industries late in your career. At the point that you sit down to prepare your career plan, you must map out how you will get to spend sufficient time in the two or three key functions, where your experience is lacking.

GDP GROWTH: Only companies with 100% market share should be allowed to set growth goals in their budgets that equal GDP growth.

GOALS: Setting the right goals is crucial though difficult. Both near-term and long-term goals have to be ambitious but achievable. If you always reach your goals and always get 100% of your potential bonus, then the goals are not sufficiently ambitious. If you never hit your goals and get no bonus, they are too stretched or your team is underperforming. The 'hockey stick budgets', where near-term goals are undemanding, and long-term goals that are unrealistic all need to be turned down every time you see them. Goals have to be demanding but realistic.

GOLF: Conducting business commonly requires informality within a confidential setting. The golf course can be a perfect solution in the sense that players of vastly different abilities (and both genders) can play a round without anybody raising an eyebrow. Golf is also good for your health! However, it is also time-consuming, which is why few CEOs have low handicaps.

GOSSIP: Becoming party to office gossip (exciting though the titbits might sound) must never be part of your networking efforts; network about what matters for the company and its people. Great leaders steer clear of office gossip and try to counter it when they hear it's going on.

GREAT LEADERS: A great leader is somebody with the capacity to develop clear and feasible strategy, build first-rate teams and execute the strategy. You must become a great leader in order to become a successful CEO.

GREED: Some people are born greedy. Others become greedy with success. Greed is obviously bad for business and must not be tolerated in business.

GREY: You should never think that decision-making is about choosing between black and white. If that were the case, there would be no market for great leaders. Great leaders are the ones that can find the best solutions in the grey area. Appreciate the nuanced picture.

GROWTH: Companies must grow and great companies also grow market share. Growth is good for all stakeholders. Growth creates new jobs, career opportunities, shareholder value and increased tax revenue, all of which benefit society.

HEAD HUNTERS: See executive search firms.

HEAD OFFICE: Spend enough time there to understand the strategy well and to be known for your achievements, but don't stay for overextended periods.

HERO: Great leaders are not heroes. They are leaders of successful teams that collectively on rare occasions stand out as heroes.

HOCKEY STICK BUDGETS: These are budgets where nearby goals are undemanding and distant goals are unrealistic. Never accept hockey stick budgets from your team.

HOPE: Management by Hope does not make a positive impact on performance. But in situations of crisis you must give your staff hope

HOW TO: Many of us have a tendency to tell our subordinates 'how to do' a given task. This is quite common amongst non-executive directors when in board meetings. Start asking 'What will you do?' as this encourages initiative and independent thought.

HUMOUR: Always remember that a bit of humour and fun in the workplace increases productivity. Sarcasm has the opposite effect. It must be avoided.

I: Certain people always use 'I' and 'me'. Use 'we' and 'us' as a rule and the first person singular only rarely.

INFLUENCE: Great leaders seek influence. Weak leaders seek power.

INITIATIVE: Great leaders take initiatives, relevant initiatives—and see them through to fruition.

INTEGRATION: Great leaders make sure that companies acquired are duly integrated into their companies. They do not leave the acquired company alone; they keep the best people and they don't over-integrate, i.e. destroy the acquired company.

INTERNAL COMPETITION: You cannot and should not try to avoid internal competition in your company. Internal competition is good as long as the individual does not compete at the cost of the team or the company. It is your job as leader to ensure that natural individual rivalry never damages the collective objectives.

INSPIRATION: CEOs draw inspiration from many sources—not by sitting behind their desks. They follow competitors, talk with all stakeholders, read management books, attend a limited number of relevant conferences, and so forth. However, they never go back to the office to copy the last thing, they have heard about. They distil and rework the ideas and use them as inspiration. Remember: leaders are leaders because they don't follow others.

INTEGRITY: If you are the CEO of a global company with tens of thousands of employees in 50 countries it is hard to ensure that a small number of people do not misbehave in spite of your values, controls and business systems. Misbehaviour in a remote place of a global company will spread over the internet instantly. If, or when, this happens, it is important for both external and internal reasons that you act forcefully by explaining what happened and what the consequences were for those who were guilty of the misconduct. You must show that misconduct is not tolerated so as to protect your integrity and prevent a recurrence.

INVESTORS: Investors are the owners of your company. If you are CEO of a listed company, it is important always to remember that you are not the owner. This applies even though, to all intents and purposes, you run the company as if it were your own. The company is owned by institutional investors, who have invested in your company because they like what you do. It is an impossible task to keep all investors happy all the time. Some only stay in for a short time anyhow. However, investors must be treated with respect, i.e. kept informed properly in a transparent way. Investors and their expectations must be managed as you must manage all of your stakeholders.

IQ: Great leaders do not have to be members of MENSA (a club open to members with an IQ above 132 on the Stanford-Binet Intelligence Scale). However, great leaders are not dumb and are characterized by exceptionally high levels of EQ (Emotional Intelligence). The combination of a good level of IQ and a very high level of EQ is found in the DNA of the vast majority of great leaders.

JOURNEY: We suggest that you think about the goals, objectives and development of your company as a journey rather than a destination. It is not meaningful to the majority of your managers, if you state that the company should grow from sales of $100m to sales of $200m over the next five years. It makes much more sense if you state that the company should grow by 15% per annum (for example) for as far into the future as possible. This will energize the organization and make managers want to contribute to the achievement of the goal.

JUDGEMENT: The ability to make good judgements is key if you want to become a successful CEO. Some have it, others do not. Your ability to make good judgements increases tremendously if you have a competent team, know your industry and your company really well and have your basic facts available. Do not ever think that you can find the truth that you need for your judgement in a spreadsheet, in a model or advise from a consultant.

KNOW YOUR BUSINESS: People with long-term success as global CEOs know their business intimately because they have worked in a number of different functions and different countries/continents before reaching the top. When the boss knows his or her business, discussions about big decisions become very objective and to the point.

KNOW YOUR NUMBERS: You always have to know your numbers well, but remember that you cannot find the truth in the numbers, no matter how much you analyse them.

KPIS: A total handful of five key performance indicators where three are quantitative and two are qualitative is enough to manage any business. This goes for every level of the organization. Obviously, there has to be a logical link between the KPIs from level to level within the organization. Going beyond five KPIs will cause you to lose focus.

LAME DUCK: A lame duck is a person on the way out of the organization. Make the transition as brief as possible in order to ensure loss of momentum in the business.

LAWYERS: You often meet the argument that lawyers will never become great leaders. Wrong! If lawyers have the characteristics of great leaders and they decide to manage as general managers and not as lawyers, they can well become great leaders.

LAZY: Successful CEOs are not lazy—they are full of energy. However, great CEOs often appear relaxed because they are in control and have great teams working for them.

LEADERSHIP COMPETENCIES: These are behaviours and capabilities that you develop during the course of your career by being in leadership situations. In order to progress to become a CEO, you need enormous learning ability; this is something quite different from ability to learn from books. The critical difference is the ability to take on-board from a whole variety of inputs. We are talking about the ability to ask the right questions; we're also talking about the ability to be very mentally agile, to switch from one subject to the next, to realize when there are certain areas that may no longer be relevant to what you're doing and to move on to new challenges and new ideas.

LEADERSHIP STYLES: There are many styles of leadership and many books are written about the subject. The styles span from 'dictatorial' to 'abdication'. Neither of these extreme styles are found in great leaders. Great leaders have a leadership style characterized by the ability to make great strategic decisions and the ability to assemble and inspire great teams to execute. Great leaders are great because they have a clear strategy and consistently deliver great results by getting the best out of people.

LEADING FROM THE FRONT: We do not think that the term 'leading from the front' characterizes the successful global leader. He or she is much more of a coach with the team. He or she is in charge of setting the team, deciding strategy and helping the team win.

LEAVERS: When people, including yourself, leave a company, a distinction is made between good leavers and bad leavers. When you leave, make sure you go as a good leaver. When people leave your organization, try to avoid having bad leavers. Never talk badly about good leavers, and find the right exit and be brutally honest when asked for references for good leavers as well as for bad leavers.

LEGACY: When CEOs get close to the time of retirement, they often want to leave a legacy, such as a new HQ, a mega acquisition (fiercest competitor), etc. Do not do this and don't let other people do it either. The legacies you should leave behind are your achievements as well as the team that is in place to carry on developing your great company.

LINEAR PROJECTIONS: Great CEOs do not assume that their companies will grow in a linear fashion forever. They do not model the development on a spreadsheet. They set goals that are demanding but achievable.

LONELY JOB: The CEO job should not be a lonely one. Great CEOs are not 'lone wolves'. Nevertheless, there will be some moments where the job of the CEO can feel lonely, as when you are formulating strategies and action that will have dire consequences for people in the organization.

LOYALTY: You must be loyal to those you work for and with; however, loyalty to your company stands over and above loyalty to individuals, should you be in a situation where you must choose between the two.

LUCK: We know that we are not the first to mention this, but the phrase 'the harder you work, the luckier you become' is so true and relevant for your career.

MAKING AN IMPACT: If you wish to become a CEO, your work must make an impact on the company. In your CV, you must have one or more real 'achievements' in each of the jobs that you have had. People who do not make a difference will not become CEOs.

MANAGEMENT JARGON: Use normal language and avoid the use of the latest management buzzwords. It is not good for your career if your people start playing Management BS Bingo when you make presentations or give speeches. The use of plain language simplifies things and eases communication. Jargon complicates.

MANAGEMENT STYLE: Your management style is critical if you want to be a successful CEO over a long time. Achieving great results is not enough. They have to be achieved with the *right* management style.

MANAGER OF THE YEAR: Avoid the nomination if you can! It is our experience that the criteria that award committees use for choosing managers of the year more often than not have very little to do with great leadership and great long-term performance. We have seen many of the 'manager of the year' do very poorly later in their career.

MBO (MANAGEMENT BY OBJECTIVES): We very much agree with the late management guru Peter Drucker who said that he did not know any other effective management concept than 'MBO (Management by Objectives)'.

MBO (MANAGEMENT BUY–OUT): If you ever become involved in a buyout situation, you must ensure that you choose a side and declare openly which side you have chosen. You cannot work for the buyer and the seller at the same time. If you choose to work with one of the potential buyers and they fail to buy, you only have one choice, i.e. to leave your job.

ME: Always use *us* instead of *me*.

MEDIA ATTENTION: When your success as a leader becomes known and you are CEO of a large company, the media will become interested in you. We all like to see our picture in newspapers and magazines — at least in the early years when everything goes well. When disappointing things happen, most of us could do without it. Therefore, our advise is that you should only appear in the media when it really matters for your company. Do not be one of these CEOs who is willing to comment on anything. Even business journalists speak disparagingly among themselves of 'media tarts'.

MEETINGS: Avoid meetings that are long, have no agenda, involve no decisions being taken, and where no records are made.

MENTOR: The right mentor (including executive search consultants), especially in your early career, can be worth his or her weight in gold. Get advise when you need to make critical decisions. Listen, but make your own decisions.

MICROMANAGEMENT: If you are a great leader, you have not become so by being micromanaged by your bosses and not by micromanaging your employees. Micromanagement does not lead to great leadership.

MISTAKES: Only people who do nothing avoid making mistakes. When you make mistakes, learn from them and never make the same mistake again, and remember to take the blame when you or your team has erred. Recognize that you do not become a great leader, if you constantly fear failure.

MOODY: Great leaders are not moody. They maintain a balanced attitude to good and bad news. Moody bosses do not create the kind of work atmosphere that gets the best out of people.

MORAL COMPASS: Whatever your position, ensure you never lose your moral compass.

MOTTO: We think that it makes good sense for companies to have a meaningful and evergreen motto. However, we do not think that CEOs should have their own personal mottos unless they are meaningful and robust, and can last for decades.

NATIONALITY: In a global business world nationality should not matter but ultimately it still does. Many companies still favour their own nationals when it comes to senior appointments abroad and in HQ. We believe that it has to do with trust and, in the past, a lack of local talent. When joining a company, we make the suggestion that you explore whether there is a glass ceiling somewhere, which down the road will limit your career prospects with the company.

NETWORK: Building and maintaining a network of relevant people is very important in your business life as well as in your private life. But remember that a network can only be sustained, if it is based on a two-way communication. If you receive, you also have to give.

NEW CEO: When a company announces that there will be a change of CEO, it is widely expected that a new CEO means a new strategy for the company. The need for a new strategy should only be there, if the company has lost its way or has no strategy. In a well-run company, the strategy may be slightly adjusted. It should be deeply rooted in the organization and does not need to be changed by a new CEO.

NGO: As the CEO of a global company you are bound to have some NGOs who for a variety of reasons take an interest in your company. Do not consider them a nuisance and don't try to ignore them. NGOs are stakeholders on behalf of society and you need to engage with them accordingly. Be nice.

NICE: It is better for your career to be nice rather than to be pushy.

NICKNAMES: Great leaders do not use nicknames that are pointed or cruel.

NO: You must have the courage to use the word 'no' in situations where you feel it is appropriate — even if some people do not immediately agree. However, you must explain convincingly your reasons for saying 'no'.

NUMBER TWO GUY: Being a number two guy can be a wonderful job, but if you dream of becoming Group CEO, you must acquire number one positions early on in your career.

NUMBERS: You have to know your numbers and you have to master your numbers, but never let the numbers master you. You rarely find the truth by going over the numbers again and again.

OBSESSION: Great leaders have passion — not obsession.

OPPORTUNISTIC: There are business situations where you have to be opportunistic. If a business opportunity that is not foreseen in your plans suddenly emerges, and your business instinct tells you that *this is an opportunity we should not miss*, then you should go for it. This should be an exception—not the rule. You may also, unexpectedly, be offered a job opportunity in your company or in another fine and relevant company which was not in your career plan. Use your judgement and instinct to make a decision. Do not just ignore the chance. Most people only get one or two 'fantastic' career opportunities in their lives.

OPPOSITION: Business is not like politics where you are either in government or in opposition. In business, everybody is in government.

OPTIMIST: Your chances of being a successful CEO increase greatly if you are an optimist.

ORGANIC GROWTH: Businesses must grow. Growth is good for all stakeholders (investors, employees, suppliers, the taxman, etc.). A sustainable business must have healthy organic growth, which can be complemented by meaningful acquisitions.

OVERCONFIDENCE: Be confident but not overconfident. Being overconfident can lead to undue risk-taking. It can also lead to very unpleasant behaviour that people around you cannot stand.

PASSION: You mostly hear about passion for people; this is, of course, something that you must have, if you want to become a great leader. However, you must also have passion for getting things done, for your company, its values, products, etc. Passion is essential. Obsession is to be avoided.

PATIENCE: Great leaders and successful CEOs are normally not very patient when it comes to performance. But during your career there are times when being patient pays off. If you feel that your next promotion is overdue, you may start looking for opportunities elsewhere. In most large organizations unexpected things happen all the time. Some degree of patience may pay off.

PAY: There will probably be times, especially in your early career, when you are unhappy with your pay. If you are on a career track that has a high probability of leading to your dream job, you should not be tempted to change for a 10% or 20% pay rise. Think about your lifetime income and you will see how little this matters. Salary increases disappoint recipients frequently. However, a constructive dialogue with your boss will go a long way to avoiding repetition. You might learn that your remuneration expectations are too high in this company; at least, however, you should also know how to improve your performance.

PERCEPTION: In a corporate environment, reality matters most but perception should not be ignored.

PERSONAL BRAND: A personal brand should encapsulate what you stand for.

PESSIMIST: Pessimists do not make great leaders.

POPULAR: Great leaders do not seek to be popular. They seek to be respected.

POWER: Great leaders do not seek power. They seek influence.

POWER COUPLES: Agreeing priorities between couples regarding work-life balance is always very important. Even more so between so-called *Power Couples* where both parties have to understand and accept that there is a price to be paid if both want to have an ambitious career.

POWER POINTS: Remember that there are times where a one-page memo with your proposal is much more efficient and appreciated than a 10-page Power Point presentation with lots of bullet points and spread sheets. The one-page report will demand much more thought, preparation time and commitment from you.

PROBLEMS: Great leaders do not procrastinate. Delaying dealing with problems often exacerbates the situation.

PROMOTIONS: You will learn that promotions do not always come when you expect them to come. Sometimes, they take longer. If so, be patient. Sometimes, promotions come earlier. If so, be happy.

PROMISES: Always keep your promises.

PUBLIC SPEAKER: 80% is about your story. 20% is about your presentation skills. Not the other way round.

PUNCTUALITY: Great leaders are punctual.

PUSHY: Be nice, not pushy.

QUALITY: Make sure that the quality of your work is high. Also in the detail.

RECRUITMENT: One of your most important tasks as a leader is to recruit people. We all have a tendency to like and recruit people who are as we are. Remember that a strong team has diversity. Not clones of yourself. Be thorough with all aspects of recruitment.

REORGANIZATION: We live in a very competitive global world. This means that there will be times when you have to reorganize. Some people see reorganizations as a threat to their position. People who want to become great leaders often see reorganizations as an opportunity to grow and learn.

RESIGNING: There are situations where the issue of resigning from a job can become relevant. The most obvious one is when you are offered a new and better job. Another far less obvious one is when you have to be brave enough to resign and move on before you are dismissed from a job in which you are not performing. You ought to be the first one to know, if you are an underperformer. The ultimate concept of resigning from a job is when a successful CEO surprises everybody by resigning early from his or her final job to pursue a second career. For chairmen and board members the issue of resigning becomes relevant when they disagree with the owners or with the majority of the board. *When* to resign and *how* to resign requires good judgement.

RESPECTED: Great leaders are respected, which is not the same as being popular.

RESPONSIBILITY: Don't be afraid of taking on responsibility.

RESULTS: The only objective way to judge executives is on their long-term results and *how* they achieve these results.

REFERENCES: If you are asked for references on someone who has worked for you there are two worthwhile principles to bear in mind: Firstly, ask about the scope and responsibility of the new job, so that you can evaluate if it is right for the candidate; and Secondly, be brutally honest. If you give a better reference than the candidate deserves, you will do nobody a favour. The candidate will get a job that he or she cannot do and will lose quite quickly. The candidate and the new employer are both losers and your own reputation will suffer. Similarly, should you request references for a CEO-candidate whom you are considering hiring, there are three worthwhile principles to consider: Firstly, explain the job in question. Secondly, ask the referee to be honest. Thirdly, obtain detailed information as to the candidate's achievements, strategic skills, leadership skills, personality, management style, etc.

RISK: Business is risky. As a leader, you are constantly faced with having to assess the risks of your decisions. Risks have to be judged and mitigated. However, you cannot run a business without taking risks.

ROLE MODELS: It is very difficult to find a role model who will be of use to you throughout your entire career. It is a bit like education: in nursery school you have nursery teachers and at university you have professors. Learning from strengths and weaknesses of your bosses and of their bosses is a very educational and effective way of on-the-job learning.

SACRIFICES: Executives who love what they do and who are in control do not feel that they make sacrifices.

SALES & MARKETING PEOPLE: You often meet the argument that sales and marketing people will never become great leaders. Wrong! If sales and marketing people have the characteristics of great leaders and they decide to manage as general managers and not as sales and marketing people executives, they can well become great leaders.

SARCASM: Sarcasm may do well in theatrical plays and stand-up comedies. Do not ever try it in business, if your ambition is to become a successful CEO.

SHAREHOLDER VALUE: You cannot create long-term shareholder value if you do not take due care of your employees, customers, the environment and the wider society. There is much academic debate about the relative merits of 'shareholder value' and 'stakeholder value'. We think that this is a rather redundant debate, because you can only produce sustained shareholder value if you treat all of your stakeholders (employees, customers, shareholders, the environment and society) with equal decency.

SHORTNESS: 'I made this letter very long because I did not have the leisure to make it shorter,' Blaise Pascal. Learn from this quotation and take the time to make your reports and presentations short and to the point.

SILOS: Many companies are organized by line of business and some by geography. Lines of business are often called 'silos' in management jargon. Moving from one line of business to another in the same company is often very difficult — or sometimes even impossible. The same goes for geography. If you spend most of your time in one particular region, you may get stuck there, if you do not make a special effort to move on.

SIMPLICITY: Great leaders keep things simple. They do not complicate.

SPECIALIST: The transition from specialist to general manager is not always easy. You may be a business controller with a high IQ who knows 'everything' about your company and how it should be managed. You may impress people with the extent of your knowledge. However, if you lack the characteristics and skills of a great leader, it would be better for you to continue your career as a specialist.

SPEED/SENSE OF URGENCY: Great organizations have an atmosphere where speed and a sense of urgency is a constant thought not to the extent of hysterical constant stress.

SPORT: It appears that team sports contribute more to development of great leaders than individual sports do.

SPOUSE: Spouses often play a very important role behind the scenes in their partner's business success. Of the many advantages of working outside your home country is the fact that your spouse, quite naturally, becomes very involved in your job. You invite colleagues and bosses to your home when they visit your business. Involving your spouse has many advantages, such as sparring, accepting and understanding your long working hours, and allowing your partner to feel more involved in the joint project that is your life together.

STAKEHOLDERS: Treat all stakeholders with respect

STORYTELLING: 'Telling stories' and 'storytelling' are two very different concepts. 'Storytelling' is a great corporate word for the ability to talk with enthusiasm and engagement about your vision for the company, its strategy, goals, values and history. 'Storytelling' is a natural skill possessed by great leaders. On the other hand, 'telling stories' is generally attached to executives who spin a good yarn but who never deliver. It is also a byword for tittle-tattle, gossip or idle talk.

STRESS: CEOs who master their jobs don't usually get stressed. CEOs who are micro managers and control freaks are much more likely to become stressed.

STRATEGY: Successful CEOs embed a strategy within the company that is deeply rooted in the organization and which creates a sense of purpose for all employees. Strategies should not come and go with CEOs.

SUCCESS: Ensure that success criteria are well defined, understood and accepted.

SUCCESSION: There are two very distinct succession issues that you may come across. The most talked about is that of CEO succession. As a CEO, you have two roles to play in relation to your own succession. One is to have a pool of competent succession candidates in place. The other is to time your departure in such a manner that a bitter fight among the candidates to succeed you is minimized. The timing issue is very difficult because there are always a few more things you would like to do. And this is very dangerous. You see many cases where CEOs want to leave legacies such as large acquisitions. A less talked about succession issue is the one that you will face five or six times in your career, i.e. every time you are promoted. Remember always to have a minimum of two members of your team who can take your job at about the right time. Also, be prepared for the unexpected promotion. Not all promotions follow the time-table. New opportunities arise when superiors leave the company.

TEAMS: Most of us have a tendency to recruit and gather people around us who are similar to ourselves. This gives us comfort and feels good. However, it is not a good way to assemble high-performance teams. Whether it is a project team or a board that has to be assembled, diversity works best. Diversity in skills, culture, gender, age and experience that collectively match the task at hand is what you need to perform well. It is unlikely that a Brazilian football team with eleven Neymars would have won the world cup.

TECHNOLOGY: Its purpose is to help people become more productive and make better decisions. You are in charge here. Do not be its slave.

THANK YOU: Use the term generously but not gratuitously.

TEMPER: Losing your temper in the office is utterly unacceptable. It betrays weakness, lack of self-control, and disrespect for your colleagues. Even if you have done it only once, you should seriously consider whether you have what it takes—and *all* it takes—to become a CEO.

TIME TO GO: There are two time to go situations for you to think about: one is at the end of your career; the other can be during your career. Both are extremely difficult to deal with, as you cannot openly talk with anybody at work about it, and you should not let anybody get the sense that you may be considering leaving your job. This is a situation where all your skills and senses will be tested. You depend on your own judgement, ideally supported by your spouse and/or a good friend. The moment your decision to go becomes known in the organization, you become a lame duck—no matter what people tell you and what you want to believe. When you have decided to go, do so with elegance. Get the timing right and make sure that you have very competent successors in place. Make the transition as brief as possible.

TITLES: Jobs are more important than titles. Some companies are very generous with titles. There are banks with more than 1,000 vice presidents. Other companies are less generous. There has also been inflation in titles over the years. The general manager first became managing director, then president and now CEO. A few choose to style themselves 'President&-CEO'. Titles are important. We want people to know who we are. Titles are important for the individual and family, in dealings with customers, suppliers, colleagues, etc. However, in the very early part of your career, you should not be obsessed as long as you do not fall behind your peers. Later in your career, when the business card carries the title CEO, it shows that there is only one like you in your company—unlike the bank with 1,000 VPs.

TRANSPARENCY: The opposite of transparency is opaqueness. It is therefore obvious that you, as a great leader, adopt a business approach of transparency.

TRAVELLING: CEOs of large global firms must consider carefully, how they most efficiently spend their time—not an easy task. If you are the CEO of a global company with 100 staff at head office and 100,000 employees in 50 countries, you have a serious dilemma. The best decision is often that you spend 40% of your time at your head office and 60% of your time travelling to visit operations abroad, customers and shareholders. And even with such a schedule, it will be difficult to visit operations in all 50 countries with the frequency that both the local country CEO and you would like. Your staff at HQ will tell you that you travel too much. There are ways to mitigate the dilemma, such as through emails, telephone conferences, video calls and management conferences. Nevertheless, you cannot run a global company without a lot of travelling.

TRUST: The opposite of trust is mistrust; therefore, it is obvious that you should always establish a climate of trust in your business. This will get the best out of your team.

UNEXPECTED EVENTS: Be ready for unexpected events—they will occur. See unexpected events as opportunities. If a CEO role suddenly becomes available in a country that is not on your list, go for it. If one of your superiors suddenly leaves, do not say no to his or her job because you feel that you are not ready for it. If you can swim, you can also swim in deep waters.

UNIONS: In many parts of the world, it is very common to dislike unions; however, unions have a role to play and they will not go away. You should therefore consider them as stakeholders and deal with them accordingly through constructive and transparent dialogue.

VALUES: Every company has its formal and informal values, i.e. 'how we do business and how we don't do business', 'what are our ethical standards?', etc. Values are created, lived and communicated by people. They are about what you do; not about what you say or write in your manuals, brochures, annual reports and so on. You must identify with the values of your company.

When considering moving to a new company, you should make a great effort to understand the values of your new employer by talking to as many people as you can to ensure that you can identify with these values. As a CEO, you are very much the role model when it comes to values.

VISION: Successful long-lasting CEOs make sure that their companies have a clear vision which becomes the 'guiding star' for the company's development and which gives each employee a clear understanding as to why his or her job is so important for the company.

VOCABULARY: You will find that use of decent language—not swearing or using dirty words—works much better than the alternative.

WE: Never use 'I' when you talk about your business and its achievements. Always use 'we'.

WHEN IN DOUBT: Benjamin Franklin's wise quote "when in doubt, don't do it" also applies to decision making in business. Especially when it is about recruitment.

WHY/WHY NOT?: Use the why/why not concept smartly and you will see that it helps you make better decisions.

WINNING: Always remember that teams should win—not individuals.

WORK—LIFE BALANCE: There are many great books for you to read about this important subject. With the heavy workload of a CEO it is our recommendation that you at each stage of your career draw up a plan together with your spouse defining your private goals, priorities and trade-offs. You can achieve a lot and can overcome a lot. But you cannot do 'everything'.

WORKING HOURS: CEOs don't usually keep time sheets. To understand what it takes to be a successful CEO we believe that most CEOs work 60—70 hours per week 46 weeks per year during their Pre-CEO career and during their CEO career. This gives a workload of about 3,000 hours per year. In their second career, the workload typically falls to 40—50 hours per week 40 weeks per year equalling 2,000 hours per year. In their third career, the workload often starts with 30—40 hours per week during 40 weeks per year, which equals 1,500 hours per year and falls to zero after 10—15 years. When your job takes so much of your time, you realize that careful planning of your work-life balance becomes extremely important.

X-FACTOR: Winners of X-factor TV competitions rarely become successful CEOs.

YES: The Yes-Boss mentality does not exist in companies with great leaders. Great leaders instill a working environment and employ smart people who are expected to express their opinions and not just say Yes to everything

ZERO—TEN SCALE: Many managers struggle with determining what is important. A simple method that we have found very helpful has been to ask the question: "On a scale from 0—10, how important is this?" When posing this question to a CEO who presented an acquisition to his board he paused for a long time, finally said "5" and then added, "I no longer think that we should make this acquisition."

CHAPTER 24

FROM LOCAL BOY
TO GLOBAL CEO

It was only after I stepped down from my last CEO job (XL) that I began to explore the discipline of leadership in more detail. I became very interested in career development, when I started lecturing about leadership to MBA students at the International Institute for Management Development in Lausanne (IMD), London Business School (LBS) and Copenhagen Business School (CBS). Stepping down from the CEO role and taking on the role as chairman of many companies opened my eyes. During my time as Executive in Residence at IMD I lectured Leadership to MBA classes and I trawled through the subject of leadership to write my first book. My third book FROM MBA TO CEO was a result at my lecturing activities.

Amongst the first things, I did when I decided to write FROM MBA TO CEO was to cast a glance backwards over my professional life. I tried very hard and objectively to analyse the opportunities that I have been given and the choices and decisions I have made.

My story was only included in FROM MBA TO CEO and again in THE JOB OF THE CEO because I was told that it gives a real life narrative including lessons, experiences and key decisions which show my credentials as a practitioner.

It was not written in the stars that I would have a CEO career. I was a very ordinary middle-class boy from a small town in Denmark.

If you were to ask my childhood friends, I do not believe any of them would have predicted I would become CEO of a major global company. The only small leadership roles I had in my early years were as a patrol leader with the boy scouts and later as Deputy chairman of the Young Conservatives Club in my home town.

As a boy, I wanted to be a medical doctor. The sight of our family doctor's car—a splendid white Ford cabriolet with a powerful V8 engine—perhaps inspired this ambition. However, as I grew older, I realized that the study of medicine was almost perpetual. By the time I reached the age of fifteen, I was very tired of going to school. I was quite proficient at math, had a good pair of hands, and was very interested in technical matters. One of my father's friends was an engineer who had his own company producing agricultural machines. He invited me to eye opening visit at his factory.I became fascinated and therefore **decided that I wanted** to become a mechanical engineer with a degree based on four years apprenticeship and a bachelor's degree.

My key lesson from my four years as an apprentice—repairing ploughs, tractors and combine harvesters—was a deep respect for people on the floor and their pride in doing a good job. I also benefitted from hands-on manual work. Work discipline was another key lesson from my period on the 'workshop floor'. We worked a nine-hour day, starting at 07:30. A long day in the repair workshop concluded with a bicycle ride home in a dirty boiler suit and with dirty hands. A very different life to the comfortable life at school among good friends and with lots of leisure time.

At engineering school, I did not get involved in the student organization. After the first year, I made a **decision** that greatly influenced my career: I **decided** to specialize in industrial engineering as I could not see myself at a drawing board in an engineering company designing valves or some such.

As a student, I kept a scrapbook. The front cover bore a photograph of an E-type Jaguar with my handwritten comment underneath, 'Therefore!' This was a memo to self-remind me that the hard grind of studying one day would reward me sufficiently to enable the purchase of this dream car.

The key lessons from my engineering studies have proven to be an important base for all my jobs. I learnt how to *plan*, *organize* and *execute*. Coincidentally, these are the elements of Peter Drucker's definition of management.

As graduation time drew closer, I made another **decision** that moved me further away from the usual engineering career track. I broadened my scope and soon hit upon an intriguing opportunity: a young and fast-growing Danish company called Dansk Chrysanthemum Kultur (DCK) with production facilities on the Italian island of Sardinia and headquarters in Denmark. Though only established four years beforehand, DCK was already Europe's largest industrial nursery and producer of flower cuttings, including chrysanthemums and carnations. The company advertised a job for an industrial engineer for its production-planning department at its headquarters near Copenhagen.

I had an interview with the general manager on a Saturday morning. After one hour he asked whether I could start on Monday, two days later. I was over the moon. I had found a very well paid dream job. I travelled back home with a signed contract; and actually only started my new job 9 days later, since I still had one subject left in my graduation exam.

I started out with the job I was hired to do—production planning at the company's headquarters, an old farmhouse near Copenhagen. From the outset, I worked very hard and put in long hours. Six months later, I was transferred to the production facilities near a beautiful beach on the island of Sardinia along with a group of young colleagues. I had just celebrated my 25th birthday when I travelled from Copenhagen Airport to Cagliari Airport, Sardinia, on a cargo DC-6 with my colleagues and a few personal belongings. Having just completed 25 years, this was my very first flight, and I was on my way to an exciting future.

I stayed with DCK for four years, and was continually given new positions with management responsibility for production, maintenance and construction, logistics, and project management. The company grew at an impressive pace, engendering a dynamic work environment with plenty of opportunities to take on new tasks; great young colleagues from other countries, in a foreign country, a different culture, and a new language to be learnt. The advantages were numerous.

An ancillary benefit for a motor enthusiast such as me was the opportunity to progress up the car ownership ladder. During my short stint at DCK HQ in Denmark I had bought my first car, which was a white Volkswagen Beetle. Though an iconic model in many respects, the only resemblance it bore to the Ford V8 cabriolet of my family doctor was its colour. In Italy, I upgraded to a white Fiat 850 Spider, a small but beautifully shaped convertible designed by the great Giuseppe Bertone. Although still a long way from the Jaguar E-type of my dreams, the Spider was perfect for a bachelor in sunny Sardinia.

After four fantastic years in Sardinia, I again made a very conscious **decision**, which influenced my life and career in a very big way: I quit my wonderful job in Italy because I had become very interested in the CEO's PA at the HQ in Copenhagen. I left my dream job in sunny Italy and moved back to Copenhagen without having a new job. My first priority was not a new job, but a young lady.

It was not without regret that I said goodbye to my sunny Mediterranean island and my colleagues. Although I had not had any formal profit and loss responsibility, I had reaped a wealth of experience from my Sardinian sojourn. I had my priorities straight and I realized that hard work and dedication were good for your career.

Back in Denmark, I was very lucky to get the girlfriend who had prompted my **decision** to return, and I had a very clear idea about the kind of job I wanted to have next. I wanted an expatriate job with a large, global Danish company. My preferred company was the EAC—The East Asiatic Company—which. At the time it was one of the largest companies in Scandinavia and a very prestigious employer. They were a shipping, trading and industrial conglomerate.

By sheer coincidence, I saw an advertisement looking for an engineer for its industrial department at the HQ in Copenhagen. This department looked after more than 100 industrial companies around the globe. Many of them were joint ventures with other groups. However, the job advertised was not the kind of job I wanted—nor was I qualified for it. Furthermore, it was based in Copenhagen. My dream was to be posted to Asia. However, as EAC rarely recruited engineers, I wanted to use this opportunity to get my foot in the door. They had a culture of only employing trainees straight from school and not of recruiting from the outside. Traditionally, chairmen, CEOs, executive committee members, country managers were all Danes who had started as trainees in EAC. I responded to the ad and was invited in for an interview. The first part of the interview was in the HR Department. I filled in the obligatory application form and went through a fairly standard interview; however, I do remember vividly that one of the questions on the form was something along the lines of, "Why would you like an overseas posting?" My answer was: "Because I think I will be able to get a management role at a younger age than if I remain in Denmark." My answer to this question turned out to be extremely significant to the way in which my life panned out. The second part comprised an interview with a deputy managing director, during which we had a great conversation. A few days later, I received a contract to work as a management trainee at HQ in Copenhagen for 12 months, after which I would be posted to an overseas company.

Although my time at EAC's head office in Copenhagen turned out to be rather shorter than anticipated originally, I nevertheless made several useful insights—not least of these was a deeper understanding of the workings of a head office, and of what was expected of the subsidiaries and their general managers.

I was, at this stage, back in Denmark, had a lovely girlfriend and a job with great overseas career potential. Expecting to stay at home for a year or so, I replaced my Italian Spider 850 with a classic red MGB roadster.

Then, quite out of the blue and just three months into the planned 12-month management trainee period, opportunity knocked: it was decided that I would be transferred to São Paulo, Brazil as General Manager (the CEO term was not used at this time) of a start-up company at the age of 29. The company was called Kemiform and specialized in the manufacturing of components for the electronics industry with a unique photochemical manufacturing technology. The prospect of becoming a General Manager at the age of 29 easily overcame my preference to avoid manufacturing industries. Nevertheless, I had one very serious issue to resolve before I would say 'yes' to going to Brazil: my girlfriend. In those days, the company dictated that you could not bring your girlfriend along on overseas postings—but you could bring your wife. This was therefore a great opportunity to ask my girlfriend and ex-colleague if she would marry me. Fortunately, the answer was yes. During the next months, I spent most of my time at Kemiform in Denmark learning everything about their manufacturing processes, cost calculations, sales and marketing, administration, etc. Eight months into my 12-month contract as a management trainee, again, my life changed in a very significant way. I married the girl I had dreamt about since my years in Italy, and I would become a general manager in a foreign country. Leaving Denmark on a snowy November day, we headed for sunny São Paulo and an incredible ten-year 'honeymoon trip' to a fantastic new country.

Over the next three years at Kemiform, we had a wonderful time. I hired and trained some great managers and staff to join our pioneering start-up company. It was a very hands-on management task in a company with only around 20 employees. Kemiform developed very well, made profits after 18 months, and I learnt an awful lot during this time. My key learnings can be summarized as full profit and loss responsibility, and everything that came with a general management position, namely strategy, budgets, execution, people and customers. I also managed to become just about as a fluent in the Portuguese language as a foreigner can become.

I got the experience of starting up a company far away from home, and I learnt to work in a hierarchy through a Country Manager to the Head Office 10,000 kilometres away.

Getting my first CEO job at an early age has been crucial for my career and enabled me to catch up with all the pre-CEO functions that I had missed in my early first job.

One of my challenges was that my bos, the EAC country manager saw me and treated me as an unwanted outsider. He did not appoint me and I was not an EAC trained person. This challenge gave me an extra reason to perform well.

During this period, I received my first company car—another white VW Beetle. Though it had no air conditioning, no sunroof and had beige plastic seats, it was still my first company car. It was not flash but it served me well in a job that required sales visits to more than 1,500 potential customers in Greater São Paulo. My wife and I also explored as much of Brazil as we could in the Beetle.

After my first three years in Brazil, I was asked to carry out a feasibility study for EAC. The project was to look at the market for contract cleaning—the daily cleaning of offices, factories, hospitals, airports, etc. EAC had entered a joint venture agreement with a Danish company called ISS—a European leader in the contract cleaning industry. The idea was to combine EAC's local know-how with ISS's industry know-how by setting up overseas 50/50 joint ventures in this particular service industry.

Contract cleaning was an industry about which I knew nothing and I had never heard of ISS. I met with the owners of the five largest players in the industry in São Paulo. The All were open to have talks about selling their companies. I prepared a feasibility study with my recommendations. After discussions between EAC and ISS, ISS's Business Development director came to Brazil for two weeks with the objective and mandate to acquire one of the five companies. We quickly identified a clear preference. By the end of the two-week visit, we had signed a letter of intent with our favourite candidate. However, well before this, the Business Development Director had told me that the partners wanted me to become Managing Director (CEO) of the company that we were going to acquire. No interview needed! I did not like the idea of working in the contract cleaning industry. I found it very primitive. It also seemed a step too far away from my engineering degree. I therefore firmly and politely, declined the offer. The business director pressed on to change my mind by talking about ISS and how it had professionalized the industry in Scandinavia. He also pointed out that the ISS group CEO as well as some of the group's senior executives, were industrial engineers. ISS was an acronym for International Service System. The word system referred to the industrial engineering business approach that ISS had adopted. During the Business Development Director's second weekend in Brazil—which he spent together with my wife and I in our home—we had both fallen for his salesmanship. He recognized this and asked me again. I **decided** to accept. This proved to be a great decision that changed the rest of my professional and my private life for the next 28 years and beyond. With the new job as Country Manager for ISS in Brazil, I stepped up from General Manager to Managing Director (CEO), and moved away from manufacturing to a very labour-intensive service industry.

After having signed the deal to acquire the Brazilian company, I travelled to Copenhagen, where I spent a fascinating month learning 'everything about contract cleaning and service management'. I worked as a cleaner between five and eight in the morning at the Technical University of Denmark in order to learn about the job on the floor. I spent the rest of the long working days at HQ, meeting people and learning what I needed to know about all key functions in the business.

After my training, I went back to Brazil and took over my new job as Managing director/Country Manager (CEO) of one of Brazil's largest companies in the industry. The company had 1,200 employees—a huge step up from 20 employees in Kemiform. I was 32 years old, and had realized my dream of getting an important management job at a young age. You can only imagine how proud I felt when I received my business card with the title *Diretor Gerente* (Managing director). I do not believe I would have become CEO of a company with 1,200 employees at the age of 32 had I remained in Denmark.

With a bigger job came a bigger company car. First a Chevrolet Opala and then a more sporty Alfa Romeo 2300ti. Both cars had 4-cylinder engines and air-conditioning. Both were based on dated European models and bore little resemblance to the Jaguar E-type; but were better than the Beetle.

I still remember the enormous weight of responsibility I felt on May 2, 1973, when I entered the door to my new company. How could little me at the age of 32 become Managing Director of such a large company? Strangely enough, I never had the same feeling in my subsequent career progression at ISS—not even when I became Group CEO 22 years later. It was an incredible feeling. But I very quickly grew into the new job.

My first priority was to recruit a management team, with whom I would develop a shared vision. I found two fantastic colleagues, an Operations Manager and a Financial Manager. The vision we developed was very simple: we wanted to be the industry leader in all aspects: professionalism, growth and profitability. Whereas many Country Managers try to minimize interactions with HQ, we decided to get a lot of assistance from some of the outstanding specialists from HQ. They came out for periods of 1—2 months in order to help train and develop local talent. We did not believe that having a lot of expatriates in the company was necessary as we were able to attract many young, talented and hard-working Brazilians to join us. One of the things of which I am most proud has been to see so many of my colleagues grow with the company. Things went very well for us. We drew attention at HQ and we evolved into a very special company in the ISS family. However, there were constant problems to overcome; high rates of inflation, poorly educated workers, changing legislation, to name but a few. It was our strategy to focus on large multinational companies as our customers. This taught us to focus on the quality of our services, which helped us to become industry leaders to the extent that our competitors poached people from us and tried to copy many of the things we did. I am very proud when people in the industry still say that we, at ISS, raised the standards of the whole industry in Brazil.

The progression from General Manager to Managing director meant reporting to a board for the first time in my career. This taught me the importance of preparing and structuring board meetings diligently. I learnt the importance of employing people with great potential and how to let them get on with the job and to grow with the company. The company we acquired was a family-owned company started by a very clever Portuguese immigrant. We successfully professionalized the company. I learnt about the importance of having a clear strategy: not to be everything to everybody. This job was a real CEO role, with full responsibility for 'everything'. It was an unbelievable experience to get the opportunity to manage a large and fast-growing company in a very dynamic market so far away from home.

After a decade in Brazil—of which seven years were spent as Managing Director of ISS in Brazil—I made another big **decision** supported by my wife. This was, once again, a move that was very important for my professional life—and certainly for our family life. I **decided** that I wanted to go back to live and work in Denmark. We enjoyed Brazil a lot, and there was more I could have done. We had a very pleasant lifestyle with many friends, a large house, pool, servants, membership of Clube de Campo de São Paulo, subtropical climate and much more. Brazil and its people are something you need to have experienced to fully understand the excitement and joy. Somehow, however, we felt we should not spend the rest of our lives there.

I informed my board of our decision very early on, so that we could prepare for an orderly succession, and I told both shareholders that I would start looking for a new job in Denmark and that I had one very attractive possibility. I felt that joining one of the two shareholders would cause problems with the other; however, both offered me a job. I accepted the job that ISS offered me, as I identified with the company knew the business from the ground. My successor was recruited and I was ready for a big move.

Back at HQ in Denmark, I became Executive Vice President (EVP) as head of Europe and Brazil, and a member of the ISS Group's Executive Management Board. I got a dream job — although not a CEO job with responsibility for 'everything'.

I came back with a truckload of fantastic experiences and memories: a 10-year honeymoon period with my wife, two children born in Brazil, and a third child made in Brazil to be born in Denmark four months after our return. Added to this was some solid career experience that had opened the door to a dream job in one of Denmark's largest and most keenly watched companies. I was 39 years old at the time — an age that suited the job.

I learnt quickly that the change from being 'The King in Brazil' to being 'A Prince in Denmark' was difficult and frustrating. Being 10,000 kilometres away from your boss is very different from having him on the floor just above you. Moving to HQ is not easy unless you become the group CEO. In fact, my new job was a shock to my system.

After some time I started to receive calls executive search firms, CEOs and chairmen with job offers. However, I always ended up concluding that the grass was probably not any greener in the other company. I always discussed these issues with my wife, and she unfailingly supported me when I **decided** to stay put.

But I was longing to become a CEO again. The only job opportunity to which I felt attracted was a CEO position in a mid-sized publicly listed company in Denmark. One of their board members recommended me to the chairman for the job. I liked the company, the chairman and all board members except one, who was opposed to my appointment. I did not get that job. With hindsight, I should be very grateful that this man did not think I was the right person for the job. Getting it would have led to a very different career for me. My move would have been a risky 'double switch', i.e. from EVP to CEO, and in a completely different industry. I did not know the term 'double switch' at the time, and seemingly did not get my risk assessment right.

My tenure at the ISS HQ also offered new motoring experiences. The best company car to which I was entitled was the Audi 100 (now the Audi 6). I had three in a row and enjoyed the top-quality, a huge improvement to my Brazilian cars.

Lessons learnt during my 10 years as Executive Vice President at headquarters:

1. HQ should be small and be the architect of strategy, financial control and allocation of financial resources. Operations should be left to operators out there in the market.
2. If you spend too long a period at HQ, as EVP or similar, you risk becoming labelled as a solid 'Number Two' man or woman, and therefore unsuitable for the top job
3. The job as EVP is far less independent than the job as Country CEO or Regional CEO away from HQ

My work situation became much better, when my boss decided to further decentralize operations. On a trip to Germany, he very surprisingly asked me, if I would move to London to do my job from there. He was in doubt, because he thought that our decision to move back from Brazil to Denmark meant that my wife and I had decided to stay there for good. I told him that it sounded very attractive indeed and that I would get back to him the next day after having talked with my wife. When I came back home from the trip to Germany late in the evening, my wife and I only needed a very short conversation, before we agreed that moving to London would be great job- and family-wise. It would be a fantastic experience for our three young children. As it turned out none of them ever returned to live in Denmark. The risk with the move was low: same company and same job, but away from the boss. Absolutely ideal.

I became Managing director (CEO) of ISS Europe Limited, which also included responsibility for our overseas operations in Brazil and later Asia. It was fantastic to have a proper CEO role again! Furthermore, I continued to be a member of the group's Executive Management Board and therefore participated in all group board meetings in Copenhagen.

After the 10 "interesting" years at HQ in Copenhagen, we moved to London. I built up a small organization with a great new team. I was 49 years old and did not at all aspire to succeeding my boss as Group CEO. I agreed with the board that I would remain in the job in London for rest of my career at the age of 65.

My company car in London was a Jaguar XJ with an 8-cylinder engine. It was not the E-type. It was not a convertible. However, it was Jaguar.

Being away from HQ and having the independence that this provided meant that things quickly started to go even better for us. We grew the business organically and through acquisitions. Profitability increased and we developed and focused the strategy. In addition, we acquired the largest Asian competitor, which then became part of ISS Europe and Brazil.

Based on my results, the Group CEO started to ask if I would be prepared to return to Copenhagen to take over his job. For quite some time I got away with politely saying that I was very happy in London, as was my family. However, after a board meeting in Geneva, he suggested that we should have a Carlsberg in Geneva Airport at Gate B34: he was returning to Copenhagen and I was returning to London. With the Carlsberg on the table, he asked formally if I would take on his job if it was offered to me. I **decided** to agree on the spot but with the caveat that it was only if the board wanted me unanimously.

When I came back to London after the Geneva trip and told my wife about the conversation with my boss, she was not at all pleased. With young children being educated in the UK, a nice lifestyle and me being very happy with my job, it was not ideal for the family; however, she agreed that I should accept if the offer came from the chairman himself.

However, things quickly became uncertain, when the board decided to conduct an internal and external search for the new group CEO through Egon Zehnder. The chairman told me not to worry: "You will be very pleased when you get the job. Not if you get the job." After conducting the internal and external search, the board did as the chairman had told me: I was appointed CEO of the group at the age of 55 with ten years to retirement. I was 29 and 32 respectively, when I was got my first two CEO roles. This was quite young. But I was quite old when I got my dream job.

When I was appointed Group CEO, I **decided** to use the title Group Chief Executive, which was a choice that stemmed from the negative associations I had with the words 'officer' and 'president'. 'Officer' to me implies commanding people rather than managing them. I find that 'President' is associated with banana republics. I therefore chose the title of Group Chief Executive. It is only after retirement that, for the sake of simplicity, I refer to myself as an ex-CEO.

The management succession plan was determined to be a 12-month transition period, during which the outgoing boss and myself, as Deputy CEO, would act in tandem. As it turned out, the transition period lasted only a few months, and I found myself in pole position much sooner than anticipated.

The negotiations surrounding my contract as CEO might be worth mentioning. When I met with my chairman to discuss it, his first question was, what did I expected in compensation. My answer was that I would like to have the same as my predecessor: whilst I suspected that he was very well paid, I did not know the numbers. The chairman said that he could not argue against my logic and I was very happily surprised, when I saw the sum involved. He then asked me about the company car: "Do you want a Jaguar like your predecessor?" Although I still dreamt about the Jaguar E-type, I declined as I felt that such a car was too flashy in Denmark. My choice was an 8-cylinder Audi A8 4.2 Quattro and the chairman approved. When I added that it cost $10,000 more than the Jaguar, he replied that he did not know that you could get cars that were more expensive than Jags. The Audi A8 4.2 Quattro was a navy blue four-door saloon—very different from the white Ford V8 cabriolet and the Jaguar E-type, but technically advanced and fantastic to drive, and so much more discreet than a Jaguar.

My appointment only happened after a very long and very unpleasant internal and external search. A barrage of newspaper articles that drew from inside information and contained much detail about the process and the individuals involved exacerbated the situation. Two of my three fellow Executive board colleagues told people that they would resign, if I were appointed. They both resigned. One of them however needed to be prompted by me. The succession was extremely badly handled, as it contravened three cardinal rules of this process: it was long overdue, it was prolonged and it was public. This created space for all manner of political manoeuvring.

My initial period as Group CEO was marred by fraudulent accounting in our US subsidiary (40% of group sales), which almost led to the bankruptcy of the entire group. We had two syndicated bank loans with 12 banks, who became very nervous. This was an extremely stressful period, and our new CFO to leave. My strategy to solve the crisis was to sell the US subsidiary. I believed that our long-troubled US subsidiary caused a 50% discount in the market capitalization of our group. We sold the business for One US$. The market liked the strategy and, as I had predicted, our market value had doubled three months later.

We started a process of developing a new group strategy along the lines of the strategy that I had successfully introduced for Europe, Brazil and Asia, whilst working in London. One of the first steps was to involve 150 top ISS executives in the process of developing a new strategy. For this, we heavily drew on the inspiration of two professors from Harvard Business School. We reorganized, we moved headquarters to more modest premises, and we acquired more than 100 companies. After five years of my tenure as Group CEO, the market value of the group had gone up six-fold.

What more could I dream for? This thought never crossed my mind until a certain Easter family holiday at our holiday apartment in the south of France. Although I was on holiday, the phone rang constantly and faxes had to be answered. My young daughter quietly let me know that, if I continued to work at this pace, I might not live as long as she would like me to. Her concern made me think and take stock with my wife. After thorough reflection I made the decision to resign five years early from my dream position. I felt that this was not only the right decision for my family and myself, but it was also the right decision for the company. However, I did not want to stop working at the age of 60: I wanted a new full-time career with a portfolio of interesting board positions and other assignments.

I handed in my letter to my chairman on a Friday afternoon at the end of July 1999 when we met for a cup of coffee, before he went away on his summer holiday. I did not tell him what was in the envelope and he did not open the letter in my presence. When he came back after his holiday, we met again. He said he knew me well enough to accept that I had made a **decision** and that he could not **make** me change my decision. Nevertheless, he tried with the whole board present; however, I stuck to my **decision** and suggested that they should consider my CFO as my successor. I knew that it was not my job to appoint a new CEO, but I saw it as my right and duty to propose an internal candidate. After some deliberation, they followed my advise. My CFO became Deputy CEO and took over from me as soon as his successor as CFO was recruited.

My key learnings as CEO are:

1. The importance of having a clear long-term strategy that is deeply rooted throughout the organization
2. Sustained shareholder value cannot be created if you do not take good care of all of your key stakeholders, namely employees, customers, shareholders and broader society
3. Succession is extremely difficult and must be managed cleverly by the board over the shortest possible period of time to avoid internal rivalry.

4. The CEO job is a wonderful job if you have a clear strategy, a strong team, a deep knowledge of your business and the right worl-life balance..

5. Arrogance is the worst enemy of great leadership whether it is something you are born with or whether you have acquired it because of your success.

6. I have used very little of my industrial engineering degree. But without this degree I would not have gotten y first job at CK and my subsequent CEO jobs!

MY SECOND CAREER: When I stepped down as group CEO of ISS, it did not take me long to have a full portfolio of great positions. Denmark is a very small country and being the CEO of a large and successful group, I became very visible. I became 'world famous in Denmark' as the Danes say.

The steep increase in our shareholder value, our clear strategy and our many acquisitions attracted the attention of the business community. Within a year, I was appointed to the position of chairman of five Danish companies and sat on five more boards. Most of these boards were supervisory boards. Over the years, I substituted some of the Danish boards with board positions of companies in the UK, Sweden, Germany, Switzerland, the Netherlands and the United Arab Emirates. I also worked with two large private equity firms.

Many other interesting opportunities opened up. I became a member of Denmark's first Corporate Governance Committee. I became an Executive in Residence at IMD in Lausanne, where I spent all my spare time during three years, writing a book with the title Winning at Service about some of my former peers whom I admired. I lectured about Leadership to MBA Classes at IMD, CBS and LBS. Other undertakings in the academic world include 10 years on the European Advisory Board of LBS (London Business School) and, since 2007, Adjunct Professor at CBS (Copenhagen Business School).

These opportunities all came about despite the fact that I had only very limited formal management training; in fact, only a one-week President's Course at the American Management Association. My management and leadership qualifications all stem from on-the-job training.

From the moment I stepped down as Group CEO, I no longer had to ask any boss or chairman as to which car I could have. Now was the time to have my dream car. Was it finally going to be the sleek 1960 E-type Jaguar which picture adorned the cover of the scrapbook from my student days? No. It had to be a more modern car but a convertible with an 8-cylinder engine. My first choice was a beautiful and very rare racing green MGR convertible, powered by the same V8 aluminium engine as in the Range Rover. Just 2,000 examples were produced. It was wonderful to drive and to own. However, unfortunately not very practical during our many trips around Europe. What I needed was a modern convertible that would also function as a touring car. The choice was easy: a Mercedes SL 500 with a V8 engine and a steel roof that folds into the boot. This is the car of my dreams — and one that I truly enjoy owning and driving. I intend to keep it or a newer model forever. The family car has been a sequence of Audi Q5 models. The present is a powerful Audi SQ5. As we live in the Alps, we also have a four-wheel drive convertible, a Mercedes Benz C43 AMG.

My key learnings from my second career are:

1. Each and every stage of a career should bring opportunities to expand one's knowledge and to learn new skills
2. The board's primary task is to ensure that the company has a clear strategy with the necessary resources to execute and that appropriate emphasis is placed on supervision and follow-up
3. The owners have the ultimate right to make key decisions. If you disagree with the owner, you have to go.

4. You must carry out very thorough due diligence before you accept board and advisory positions. Having one 'problem' position in your portfolio is like having one rotten apple in your fruit basket. Your personal brand will be destroyed forever. With this in mind, I have turned down many offers

5. You must spend a lot of time with all stakeholders to understand the role, expectations, strategy, key priorities, authority, etc., and have stated this clearly in an engagement letter to the owners and other key stakeholders

6. Ex-CEOs probably do a better job as chairmen than they do as ordinary board members.

7. Managing your work-life balance is at least as important in the second career as it was in the first.

MY THIRD CAREER: My second career came to a natural end when I turned 70. Non-executives in European companies must retire from boards when they turn 70 or when they have served on a board for 9 years in the UK and for 12 years in Europe. It was very easy for me deciding to continue being active with a third career rather than retiring. I still like to take initiatives and work with interesting people. It did not take me long to rebuild my portfolio. I am chairman of a great company in Asia, an active shareholder in three start-up companies in Asia and in Europe, I advise companies and individuals, I write books, I give speeches, i am a goodwill ambassador for Copenhagen and i help an NGO, etc. My present workload is reduced to about 1,500 hours per year, which corresponds to a full time job in many countries. We live in Switzerland and have a wonderful mix of work and active out-door life. We have second home in Denmark. We spend wonderful time with family and friends in both homes. My activities are very exciting and one thing is certain: I shall never stop being actively involved in exiting projects.

FINAL REMARKS: When I graduated as an industrial engineer, formal career planning, creation of personal brands and having a mentor were not common practices; I guess that some of us must have had some kind of dream or vision that helped us shape our careers.

I cannot say that I have benefitted directly from my degree in industrial engineer. But it has become very clear to me that I would not have gotten the jobs in DCK, EAC and ISS without the degree. And perhaps I would not have designed the career path chart that I have used so extensively in the book?

I have not had a mentor or a role model during my career. Nevertheless, many people around the world have inspired me. My three bosses have all had enormous influences on the way my career has developed, but I do not regard any of them as mentors per se. A very significant influence on my professional life has been more than 25 times participation at World Economic Forum's annual meetings in Davos, where I have met many of the world's most admired leaders and learnt valuable lessons from observing their rise and their fall. Unfortunately, many of them destroyed their careers. They became arrogant 'celebrity CEOs' who did not believe that normal rules should apply to them. That is however an entirely different, yet educational story.

Arguably, the single most important thing that I have learnt over the course of 50 years in leadership roles is that it is incredible what people can achieve, if they are given the opportunity.

Finally, influences from many sources have shaped my career, and whilst I am loath to name individuals, I make one exception to the rule: my wife, Britta. She has been a fantastic mentor in everything I have done in my private and in my professional life; someone who has helped and supported me on my journey 'From local boy to global CEO'. She is my best friend and continues to inspire me.

THE CEO CAREER PATH CHART: WALDEMAR SCHMIDT

FUTURE CEOs	PRESENT CEOs	RETIRING CEOs
AGE: 25–29	AGE: 29–60	AGE: 60–80+
WORKING HOURS/YEAR: 3,000	WORKING HOURS/YEAR: 3,000	WORKING HOURS/YEAR: 2,000 ➔ 1,500 ➔ 0
YEARS IN JOBS:	YEARS IN JOBS:	YEARS IN JOBS:
KNOW YOUR CUSTOMERS: ☐ Sales ☐ Marketing ☐ Customer service	CEO JOBS: ☑ S – Small ☑ M – Medium	SECOND CAREER: ☑ Chairman role ☑ Board member ☑ Other roles
KNOW YOUR PRODUCTS: ☑ Operations ☑ Manufacturing ☑ Supply chain ☐ Technology	☑ L – Large ☑ XL – Extra large ☐ XXL – Forbes Global 2000 company	THIRD CAREER: ☑ Board roles ☑ Investor ☑ Mentor ☑ Speaker & writer ☑ Pro-bono roles
KNOW YOUR NUMBERS: ☐ Accounting ☐ Business control ☐ Management consultancy (Strategy and operations) ☑ Junior management positions	AN UNEXPECTED EVENT MAKES YOU: ☐ CEO – because you were there as CFO, COO or board member	RETIREMENT: ☑ Pro-bono roles ☑ Investor ☑ Mentor ☐ Other: ☐ No more business roles

© 2020 Waldemar Schmidt

ABOUT THE AUTHOR

Waldemar Schmidt, a global businessman with considerable experience as CEO and chairman of companies from a wide range of industries across 3 continents.

Waldemar got his first CEO job when he was 29 and progressed to become CEO of ISS, the Copenhagen-based global facility services group (XL) that is amongst the largest corporate employers in the world.

Waldemar is born on 4th July 1940 in a small town in Denmark. He has lived and worked outside Denmark most of his working life in Italy, Brazil, UK and Switzerland.

Whilst managing ISS's business in Brazil, he received the Danish Export Oscar. In 2000, the Queen of Denmark awarded Waldemar the Order of the Knight of Dannebrog and promoted him to Knight of Dannebrog 1st Degree in 2008. In 2006, he was awarded the Order of the Polar Star by King Carl XVI Gustaf of Sweden.

All royalty income from the sale of THE JOB OF THE CEO goes towards Waldemar Schmidt's scholarship for foreign MBA students at CBS—Copenhagen Business School, Denmark.

PREVIOUS BOOKS
BY THE AUTHOR

WINNING AT SERVICE—LESSONS FROM SERVICE LEADERS: Is about how four European service companies became world leaders in their industries: Compass and Sodexo in the catering industry; and Securitas and Group4Falck (Now G4S) in the security industry. WINNING AT SERVICE was written by Waldemar Schmidt while he was an Executive in Residence at IMD in Lausanne, Switzerland in cooperation with IMD, McKinsey and Egon Zehnder. Published by Wiley in 2003.

DENMARK LIMITED—GLOBAL BY DESIGN: Denmark Limited tells how Denmark has managed to become a very competitive industrial nation with well-known global companies such as LEGO, Carlsberg, B&O-Bang & Olufsen, Maersk, NovoNordisk and hundreds of hidden champions, who are global leaders in their fields. Published by GAD in 2006. The authors are Waldemar Schmidt in his capacity as Goodwill Ambassador for Copenhagen assisted by Clare McCarthy and a number of great contributors.

FROM MBA TO CEO—THE JOB OF THE CEO AND HOW YOU GET IT: This book is a result of Waldemar Schmidt's extensive activity in teaching leadership to MBA students at leading business schools. The big question that the MBA students asked was: *"How do I become a CEO, What does it take and do you think that I have got what it takes?"* The lecturing and the interaction with the MBA students inspired Waldemar Schmidt to write FROM MBA TO CEO in co-operation with Egon Zehnder, the world's leading privately held global search and talent management consultancy and 200 MBA students. Published by Editora Val de Mar in 2013.

LESSONS LEARNT ABOUT THE JOB OF THE CEO

1 THE JOB OF THE CEO is a wonderful job, if you master it. But if you do not, it is very stressful

2 Getting THE JOB OF THE CEO is hard. Keeping the job of the CEO is even harder. Retiring from the job of the CEO is probably the hardest of all

3 THE JOB OF THE CEO is a high reward/high risk job with an average tenure of 3 – 5 years

4 If you lose your CEO job once you should try again. But if you lose 2 or more CEO jobs you are better advised to reorient your career

5 CEOs are rightly judged on the results they achieve. But HOW they achieve their results is also important

6 Knowing your numbers is essential, but not enough. Knowing your products and services is essential, but not enough. Knowing you customers is essential, but it is not enough. If you want to be a successful CEO over a very long period, you must know and be interested in your numbers, your products and services, your customers; and all other key stakeholders

7 Great leaders act like playing coaches with their teams

8 Arrogance is the worst enemy of great leadership whether you are born arrogant or whether you have become arrogant as a result of your succes

9 THE JOB OF THE CEO and the pre-CEO jobs are 24/7 jobs with 3,000 working hours per year.

10 The big work-life question at all times during your career is, whether you can have a long and successful CEO career and at the same time have a happy family life? The answer is YES! But only if you and your spouse plan your work-life balance in the same diligent manner as you plan your career and only if you master your CEO job. We argue that it is very difficult or perhaps even impossible to have a long and successful CEO career without also having a happy family life